TAKING AIM

TAKING AIM

Daring to Be Different, Happier, and Healthier in the Great Outdoors

EVA SHOCKEY

with A.J. Gregory

CONVERGENT

NEW YORK

Published in the United States by Convergent Books, an imprint of
the Crown Publishing Group, a division of Penguin Random House
LLC, New York.
crownpublishing.com

CONVERGENT BOOKS is a registered trademark and the C
colophon is a trademark of Penguin Random House LLC.

Library of Congress Cataloging-in-Publication Data is available
upon request.

ISBN 978-0-451-49927-1
Ebook ISBN 978-0-451-49928-8

Printed in the United States of America

Names in Chapter 6, "Holding Your Own," have been changed to
protect the privacy of the participants.

Title page photo by Josef Hanus / Shutterstock
Jacket design by Jessie Bright
Jacket photograph by Shawn Wagar

10 9 8 7 6 5 4 3 2 1

First Edition

To my family—the originals and the new—you are my life

CONTENTS

> > > > > > > > > > > > > >

CONTENTS

INTRODUCTION

Nobody says a word. A reverent quiet cradles the great Yukon stretching around us. I walk silently, strategic with every step of my well-worn hiking boots, trying to avoid dry twigs and leaves. Cool wind rustles the scrub willow. We're tracking the long, narrow grooves of hoofprints freshly pressed into the soft ground. They're each the size of my hand from wrist to fingertips. I know he's close.

Step.

Pause.

Step.

Crunch.

My eyes scan the landscape, which swells from deep valleys where streams bubble to rolling hills topped with skinny willow runs. *Where is he?*, I wonder, hoping to glimpse the telltale, satellite-dish-like antlers sticking out of the brush. Walking through the six-foot-tall willow grove makes it hard to spot anything.

But then I hear him.

The low grunting is unmistakable, maybe only a hundred yards away, but I still can't see anything through the willows. I make my way through the scrawny brush, watching, waiting. Careful not to let a branch smack me in the face or a twig snap underfoot, I inch ahead, following Dad, who is doing the same. Finally, I catch a glimpse of massive antlers. The bull moose is slowly making his way up a small hill. It's him. My heart beats faster, the adrenaline kicking in. As the bull continues to make his way up the hill ahead of us, more and more of his ungainly and massive brown-haired body comes into view.

About seventy-five yards away now, the moose stands tall. Swaying back and forth as the wind crackles through the trees, he lowers his head, his grand spread of antlers disappearing into the brush. Dad cups his hands together over his mouth and grunts softly, expertly mimicking another bull trying to encroach upon territory that's not his. If it works, the moose we're watching will come closer, intent on establishing dominance.

But the moose doesn't budge.

It wasn't that long ago that I would have stood on the same spot, watching the same animal, without a clue about what I was supposed to do next. But on this day, I know what to do. The window of opportunity is closing. I have to act fast.

I set up the shooting sticks, resting my rifle in the crook of the V. Shooting with accuracy and precision isn't easy even in the calmest of situations, let alone when you're staring down a gun barrel at a live animal. In order to have the best chance at a good, clean shot, it's best to rest your firearm on something, whether a mound of dirt, a tree limb, or a backpack. Shooting sticks (the brand I use are called Primos Trigger Sticks) do the job.

With a deep exhale, I release tension from my body, counteracting the adrenaline now rushing through my veins. With the crosshairs settled behind the bull's shoulder, I squeeze the trigger in slow motion. The shot cracks the air, rolling echoes all around and sending shivers up my spine. Then, silence. I see only willow.

The shot is good.

> > >

As a little girl with dreams of becoming a ballerina, never would I have imagined that I'd be scaling rugged mountains and glassing* deep valleys for a fifteen-hundred-pound bull moose. And I couldn't have imagined the thrill of it. Not in my wildest dreams.

I've always loved the maxim "Man plans. God laughs." It's how this story begins. Ever since I can remember, I'd gone on hunting trips with my father, a world-class hunter and creator of the TV show *Jim Shockey's Hunting Adventures*. A pioneer in the hunting-media industry, Dad has traveled the world to film his adventures. As a professional big-game outfitter, he owns the guiding rights in several exclusive

---

* Glassing means looking through binoculars or a scope to find wild game.

hunting territories across Canada, so he and others from our family business guide fellow hunters on excursions of their own. I was proud of Dad, but that didn't mean I planned to join his ranks. I didn't "get" hunting and had zero desire to even try it. My friends thought it was plain weird to abandon the convenience of a grocery store and the comforts of home to spend days in the wilderness, cold, wet, and tired, for the mere possibility of harvesting an animal—and, frankly, so did I.

But once I got it, I never looked back.

Today, hunting is one my passions, handed down to me through generations of hunters on both sides of my parents' families. I was fortunate to go on many hunts with my mom's father, Grandpa Len, and Dad's father, Granddad Hal, before they passed away. These men truly appreciated and exemplified the joy and passion of hunting and filling their families' freezers with wild game. Not to mention that they had a lot of fun in the process. It was an honor to share this pastime with two great men.

Contrary to what I thought at first, hunting isn't easy. No one warned me how uneventful some hunts would be. Or how bitterly cold. Or how much hiking might be required. Or how much I'd need to practice shooting, whether with a gun or a bow. I, too, assumed, much to my naïveté, that a hunt was simply about killing an animal. Period. End of story. In this book, I share how I came to realize that the harvest is but a small piece of a larger puzzle. Hunting encompasses every single moment leading up to the one in which you take the shot. Like the training, the hours upon hours spent practicing your craft. Like the time and the money that go into pulling off a successful hunt. Like the incredible memories made. Like the fresh air of the great outdoors that invigorates you and forces you to breathe, really breathe. Hunting is also about the moments that follow the shot: the skinning, the gutting, the butchering, and the cooking of wild game that eventually satiates your senses with every mouthwatering bite, making the bone-chilling cold, the achy muscles, the grime, and the fatigue all worth it.

I read somewhere that "An arrow can only be shot by pulling it backward." In other words, anything worth doing in life will come with resistance. You may hunt. You may not. But if you've worked hard to achieve a goal or a dream or are right now in the midst of fighting for or striving for something you believe in, you can relate to the challenges I've faced. You know what it's like to go up against the status quo. You know the discipline required, the struggle that follows. You know the detours. You know the critics who tell you to quit or that you'll never make it. You know the self-doubt that creeps in. And one day you'll know what it feels like when you wake up and realize that you've created your own life, your own future, and left your own mark on this world.

My story is not solely about hunting nor intended only for would-be hunters. It's for all you women and girls who yearn for a life full of adventure. It's about discovering your dream, following your personal passion, mastering your skills, taking aim no matter who thinks you're crazy . . . and then letting the arrow fly. If you've done all you can, I can tell you from my own experience that you're almost certain to hit your mark.

My decision to hunt was met with opposition that grew over the years. Friends thought I was crazy. Strangers assumed I was in it to get a trophy animal. A few guides pegged me as a diva or spoiled brat before even meeting me. I've walked into hunting camps where I could tell that some of the guys were wondering who invited the girl. Anti-hunters have sent me death threats. I've been told in myriad ways— some more creative than others and many in colorful and coarse language—that I'm in the wrong place doing the wrong thing, that hunting is evil and I am evil for doing it.

Yet humans have hunted since the beginning of time. Millions of years ago, it was about using a slingshot, spear, or stick and string in order to eat and survive. Today, in the modern world, hunting has evolved in many ways, both good and bad. It pains me to hear of people who hunt illegally or of poachers who exploit wildlife to make a buck. I am part of a community that understands that hunting is about so much more than mere sport. For instance, it's truly conservation-oriented. Does that surprise you? Hunters currently raise more money for conservation of our natural resources and for wildlife management than does any other group on the planet. Hunting is also about a deep appreciation of nature. Sitting in a tree stand or hiking to the top of a mountain invites one to breathe deeply of fresh air and admire all of God's beautiful creations. Hunting is now about unplugging, too, turning off phones, computers, and social networks in favor of spending quality time in the natural world with the ones we love. Finally, hunting is about feeding our families. Hunters know where food comes from and are grateful for the animals that give their lives to nourish our bodies.

Another way that hunting is changing is that the world is finally recognizing the emergence of women hunters in what was previously viewed as an exclusively masculine pursuit. Which is odd, when you think about it, because famous women hunters have been around forever. Artemis, the ancient Greek goddess of the great outdoors, was, like today's hunters, both a hunter and protector of animals. Her Roman counterpart, Diana, goddess of the hunt and the woodlands, was often pictured with a bow and quiver. Dozens of centuries later came the gun-toting Annie Oakley, a petite woman often referred to as "Little Sure Shot," who said, "God intended women to be outside as well as men, and they do not know what they are missing when they stay cooped up in the house."[1] Today we can appreciate such legends as Brenda Valentine, the "First Lady of Hunting," the only woman to ever receive the Knight Rifle "Master Hunter" award; and Mary Cabela, who, alongside her husband and his brother, helped start and build a world-famous hunting, fishing, camping, boating, and shooting retail empire.

These women are pioneers of hunting, heroes who have inspired thousands of girls to pick up a gun or bow and head for the great outdoors. In 2001, only 10.2 percent of hunters were female. By 2014, the number had jumped 84 percent, to 3.3 million female hunters. The number of women bow hunters is even more impressive. In that same time span, the number grew 167 percent, to almost 1.1 million.[2]

I've been blessed to be surrounded by amazing and talented hunters who share my passion for the lifestyle. Among them is Tiffany Lakosky, who hosts one of the most popular hunting television shows on Outdoor Channel and who has changed the game for women hunters in the last decade. Another inspiration for me has been a well-known fitness/ nutrition expert and non-hunting vegetarian I met two years ago who became an impassioned bow hunter when she realized how healthy organic wild game is to fuel our bodies. Another friend of mine continued hiking up mountains and hunting until she was nine months pregnant! And a mom of four daughters I met at a trade show once told me that, in the absence of any hunting influences, she had taken it upon herself to learn about the lifestyle and teach her girls the wonders of the great outdoors and the importance of knowing where their meat comes from.

We hunters may look different from one another, come from different backgrounds, live in different places, use a bow or a rifle, have different preferences for gear, strategies, or styles, hunt five thousand miles away from home or in our own backyard, but we are one and the same. We are hunters.

> > >

For reasons you'll discover in this book, it was a day to remember. A little over four hours after my shot rang out in the Yukon's wild kingdom, I sat on soft, moss-covered earth before a campfire that popped and snapped. Glowing embers danced as I chewed on pieces of blackened moose backstrap, a prime cut of meat along the spine of the animal. I thought about my upcoming wedding, and with a smile on my face, I felt my heart swell with pride. The meat from this bull was going to feed my wedding guests.

I love the hunting lifestyle with an unbridled passion. I hope my journey inspires you to stretch yourself and uncover what you love to do—and then to do it, no matter the obstacles you encounter. Whether your dream is to write a book, have a family, help cure cancer, or stock your fridge with wild game fresh from the field, I hope my adventures remind you that, with effort and dedication, the life you want to live can be yours.

1

MY NORMAL

A ship is always safe at the shore—but that
is not what it is built for.[1]

—JOHN SHEDD

VANCOUVER ISLAND, CANADA, 1995

"I've got a surprise for you," Mom excitedly said to my brother and me. Strapped tightly in the back of the minivan, Bran and I cheered in unison. *It has to be ice cream,* we thought. Mom was such a health nut, this frozen treat was reserved only for rare and special occasions.

As we pulled up next to the carport, though, Mom revealed that she had an even better treat in mind: "Surprise! Daddy's home!"

Dad had been away on a moose hunt with my grandfather and uncle and wasn't expected to return for another week. My seven-year-old self tore out of that van so fast, my glossy black Mary Janes barely came to a complete stop before almost tripping over the hundred-and-fifty-pound hindquarter of a butchered moose. The meat gleamed red, marbled with fat, and rested on an orange tarp laid across the carport floor.

"Daddy!" I squealed, arms outstretched.

Dad put down a blood-splattered knife and scooped me up. "I missed you so much, Eve," he said, a twinkle in his eye.

I snuggled against Dad's heavy apron. It was stained red in places and flecked with tiny pieces of moose flesh and fur. I remember, nestling my head in the crook of his neck, that I was suddenly overcome with the scent of raw meat. "Eww, Daddy. You smell stinky!" I said, giggling. But it didn't really matter to me. I was so happy to see him, I wouldn't have cared if he smelled like sewage.

Certain memories stick with us over time, clues from our childhood that point to where we are today. Many times these memories stem from something we saw our parents do, such as working double shifts to put food on the table or studying night after night to finally earn a college degree. Or they might bring us back to a time when our parents challenged us to be all we could be. Maybe they pushed us to try out for the school play or refused to let us quit the soccer team. We might not know it at the time, but those moments wield power to shape us. As the years pass, they lead us to do certain things, go certain places, or make certain decisions . . . ones that can ultimately change the course of our lives. And it's only when that happens that we realize just how poignant those memories are.

So, back to that carport.

Dad peppered me with questions about school as he leaned against one of the counters lining a wall. My attention was so wrapped up in our conversation, I barely noticed that the carport looked like a slaughterhouse. Mounds of raw moose flesh were piled everywhere. Thick slabs of backstrap and tenderloin lined one side of the long tarp. Three massive hunks each of hind and front quarters, rich red, claimed most of the space in the middle. Clearly, the hunt had been successful, providing an entire bull for each hunter, which meant enough meat for all our families for the rest of the year.

This scene might have been out of the ordinary for most kids, but it was just another day in the Shockey household. Before I started visiting friends after school, I didn't realize that carports were called that because they were intended to shelter parked vehicles.

But "normal" is relative, right?

Our family lived on Vancouver Island, Canada, known for its rugged beauty and protected parkland. Here, the great outdoors rule. You can watch pods of orcas glide past limestone cliffs, soak up sun on a remote beach, and hike through old-growth forests where ancient trees seem to touch the sky. Much of the island is unspoiled, brimming with wildlife. Everywhere, it seems, Mother Nature is at her best.

Though my parents met and married in the city of Vancouver on the mainland of British Columbia, they wanted to raise a family with more greenery than concrete surrounding them. A place where their kids could fall asleep to the sound of chirping crickets, where they could chase frogs, pick berries, and swim in a lake right in their own backyard.

But, I'm getting ahead of myself. Let's start from the beginning.

Dad grew up in the suburbs of Saskatoon, a city in the Canadian province of Saskatchewan. From digging up earthworms when he was two to trekking through the backwoods when he was fourteen, stalking white-tailed deer with his dad, he's always been a hunter at heart. A competitive water polo player during and after university, he became the captain of the British Columbia men's water polo team, and was scheduled to compete in the 1980 Summer Olympics in Moscow. However, in protest against the Russian invasion of Afghanistan, Canada, along with several other countries, boycotted the Olympics that year. Disappointed, the team stayed home. After dabbling briefly in real-estate development, Dad tried his hand at another passion and opened an antiques and folk art store, which, over the years, expanded into three more shops.

A good-looking and charismatic guy, Dad had no trouble finding beautiful girls to date. He just couldn't find "the one." That is, until he showed up one night at the dance class Mom taught, hoping to meet a pretty girl.

Louise Johann was a triple threat: a professional ballet-jazz dancer who also modeled and acted. A gorgeous blue-eyed blonde, she was used to getting asked out by celebrities and politicians. For Dad, it was love at first sight. After class that night, Mom was looking for a ride home, and Dad happily obliged. On the drive, after small talk turned into deep conversation about how important their families were to each of them, he asked her out. Mom very sweetly said no. But that was a word my father was not accustomed to hearing; he's a pretty persistent guy. Six months later, they were married. It was a match made in heaven, although strange in a way, considering that Mom was a strict vegetarian at the time they met and Dad loved to hunt.

In their early days together, Dad focused on his antiques business. He hunted only three or four times a year—just enough to keep the freezer packed with meat—but it was clearly his passion. When he wasn't working or hunting, Dad was reading outdoor magazines. He noticed that although those periodicals featured plenty of hunting how-to articles—for example, how to form a hunting club, employ the best decoy strategies, or stay warm in a blind in the cold—they rarely offered captivating stories about individuals' adventures. So he began writing about *his* experiences in the wild, the magazines picked up his stories, and readers loved the way he packed his articles with color, emotion, and humor.

In 1986, my brother Branlin (Bran, as my family calls him) joined the Shockey crew, and two years later, I arrived. When I was around three months old, Ralph Lauren walked into one of Dad's antiques stores; it was located in the trendiest part of Vancouver. Enthralled by the beautiful, one-of-a-kind furniture and folk art, the world-famous designer bought out the entire inventory. Every. Single. Thing. While it would take a few years before Dad would start his hunting business, that remarkable transaction allowed him to purchase a commercial property on Vancouver Island, where he opened a new store. He also purchased a magnificent piece of land on the southern part of the island that included a beat-up farmhouse—our new home.

While the dilapidated structure wasn't much to look at, the land was extraordinary and a child explorer's dream. A half-mile-long gravel driveway peppered with potholes led the way to twenty-four acres of lush greenery splashed with the bold colors of wildflowers. Golden hayfields and ancient, majestic Garry oaks also dotted the landscape. Our backyard swept down to a sparkling lake, the opposite shore of which lapped quietly at the foot of a mountain.

I know—it sounds like a Hallmark movie. But I'm not making it up; our home was really like that.

My father, with the help of his dad, Granddad Hal, and Mom's dad, Grandpa Len, transformed the dilapidated farmhouse into an eye-catching sanctuary, laying down rich hardwood flooring and building intricate stone fireplaces. They also tacked on an addition: Dad's office-slash-mancave. Over the years, Dad filled the walls of this room with hundreds of taxidermy mounts from animals he harvested all over the world, to the point that barely any wood paneling is visible today.

Above his office, Dad built Mom a dance studio where she could continue her teaching. When I was eighteen months old, so I'm told, I'd sit on the shiny wooden floor, watching little girls with tight buns and pink tutus navigate their way through pliés and pirouettes. When I was two, I wanted to do more than merely observe. So, donning my own pink leotard and tutu and sporting a fairly sizable potbelly, I pranced around in my blond bowl haircut with the rest of the class.

Living where the great outdoors was celebrated complemented my parents' healthy lifestyle—and downright radical commitments. Each year, their goal was to live for twelve months without having to buy meat and produce from the store. With the smattering of fruit trees, the fifty or so rows of rectangular raised beds that grew a variety of vegetables, and Dad harvesting meat, most years it was mission accomplished.

My mom championed the benefits of organic food long before that became a trend. Thanks to Dad's hunting excursions, three or four of our huge freezers were stocked from top to bottom with wild game carefully wrapped in pink freezer paper and labeled with the cut of meat. Deer, elk, caribou, moose—you name it, we probably had it in stock. The meat was lean, free of hormones, pesticides, GMOs, and antibiotics, and she knew exactly where it came from. More important for us kids, every meal, from moose steaks to deer fajitas, was delicious! My parents taught us the basic premise of the circle of life, that humans are carnivores by nature, and to understand that whatever animal was on our plate had given its life to provide us our sustenance.

I spent a ton of time with Mom in the kitchen, where she made practically everything from scratch. While other kids were chewing on prepackaged fruit roll-ups during snack time at school, I reached into my lunchbox for homemade fruit leathers made in our own dehydrator, a piece of equipment Dad also used to make deer jerky.

So, as you can see, nothing too out of the ordinary. Normal.

People who have seen him on TV often ask me what it was like to grow up with Jim Shockey as my father. Though I didn't know it as a child, Dad was a pretty big deal. A world-class hunter, throughout the last forty-plus years, he's traveled to forty-five countries and six continents hunting all sorts of wild-game species and documenting his experiences on film.

In the process, he's accumulated a lengthy list of awards. Of course, he was always just Dad to me. And if you've never seen his show, he may be just another guy to you. The truth is, I didn't realize Dad was any different from John Smith or Billy Brown. He had a job, took us fishing, attended our sporting events, and taught us how to throw a baseball. He did what all the other construction worker, Realtor, or doctor dads seemed to do.

Then again, I never saw a deer carcass hanging in anyone else's carport. Or a skull and antlers boiling in a pot on a friend's kitchen counter. Or smelled the skunky stink of muzzleloader cleaner wafting through a neighbor's house.

And then there were the Shockey vacations. When my friends would return from a family trip, they'd brandish photos of Disney World, cruise ships, and tropical beaches. But that was not our style. Dad would hitch our oldie but goodie trailer, complete with wood paneling and plaid upholstery, to the back of the trusty 1980s-era Dodge truck, and the whole family would embark on an adventure to God knows where. But whether we were driving toward the jungles of Mexico or the mountains of Alaska, every "vacation" was a hunting trip in disguise. We spent countless nights in pup tents with rocks digging into our backs or on cramped bunks in our camper. For the other kids I knew, "camping" meant driving a luxury motor home (equipped with a shower, flat-screen TV, and a satellite dish on the roof) twenty minutes down the highway into a fully equipped campground, then putzing around on leisurely walks and eating s'mores over a bonfire at night. Our family did things a bit differently.

On one of our hunting trip–vacations when I was seven, we drove up the Alaska Highway headed toward the far northwest corner of British Columbia. Destination: the Tatshenshini River area, home to white-water canyons, snowcapped mountains, and some of the largest glaciers in the world. Dad was looking for moose, which meant that he and my brother planned to spend a good portion of the day hunting, and Mom and I would remain near the campsite exploring the scenic wildlife. Periodically, Dad would ask if I wanted to join him and Bran, but I was never interested. It didn't seem like something that the girly-girl I was at the time should do. I preferred to hang out with my mom, the textbook example of beauty and femininity.

But on this particular adventure, I discovered a new talent. One evening before sunset, Dad, his wild, shoulder-length hair blowing in the breeze, hollered, "Shooting competition!"

Bran's eyes lit up. "I'll get the cans!" he shouted, hightailing it toward the orange bag by the camper door. After he lined up some of the cans on a fallen log, Bran declared, "I'm going first," and he reached for the .22 rifle in Dad's hand. I remember what happened next unfolding something like this.

I bulldozed between the two guys. "No, me!" I insisted. Though I'd sometimes shoot a pellet gun for target practice with Dad and Bran in our backyard, just for fun, and though I'd watched my dad and brother at the shooting range, this would be my first time shooting a real rifle.

"Here, let me hold the barrel for you, Eve," Dad said. I

resisted that, too, at first. I wanted to do it myself. I realized quickly, however, that I wasn't strong enough to do it myself. Patiently, Dad showed me how to hold the gun's stock tightly against my shoulder, then rest the barrel on top of his two strong, outstretched fingers. It was a fatherly version of shooting sticks.

Guided by careful instruction, I slowly squeezed the trigger. The shot rang out, followed by a *dink* as the can I was aiming for fell off the log. A feeling of surprise rushed over me, quickly followed by pride and the urge to keep shooting.

"You're a natural, Eva!" Mom said as she gave me a high five. Dad, too, was impressed. "Holy moly!" he said. "Look at you shoot!"

All four of us then took turns and kept score. Not to brag or anything, but I won the competition.

At that age, though, I didn't have a passion for shooting. My real passion? That was for dance.

Oh, to move like my mom! She was so fluid and graceful, whether she was teaching ballet, whipping up elk burgers in the kitchen, or working deep in the soil planting vegetables in our garden. I studied dance under my mother until I was seven and then moved on to a local dance school for traditional and competitive training. I loved every second of it.

Mom's world of dance and Dad's passion for the great outdoors created a unique lifestyle for the Shockey family, in which the rugged and the delicate constantly brushed elbows. Despite the stark contrast between the two, somehow it worked. Mom supported Dad in his adventures, and Dad did the same for Mom. In hindsight, I see that I was a lucky girl. I had the rare opportunity to observe and participate as much or as little as I wanted in two totally different spheres of being.

Ever since Ralph Lauren had scooped up his entire inventory, Dad had started going on more hunting trips. In the spirit of togetherness and whenever possible, the rest of us, including grandparents, would drive to meet up with him toward the end of his trip.

Going to see Dad at bear camp at the northwestern coast of Vancouver Island was pretty fun. Of course, casually mentioning "bear camp" to my friends at school would elicit wide-eyed horror and speechlessness. But to me, going to bear camp simply meant reuniting with Dad in his outfitting territory. And if you're wondering, yes, the area is crawling with bears. Back then, the Shockey bear camp was an abandoned logging shed with a dirt floor and an un-walled rusty toilet sitting in a corner. At least it was big enough that we could pull our truck and camper into it to sleep.

My childhood was full of family trips. We took a two-thousand-mile road trip from Vancouver Island down to Mexico, where I boldly volunteered to eat raw clams from a local fisherman and won the family record for throwing up the most in twelve hours (thirty-seven times, thank you very much). I remember praying for dear life as Dad maneuvered our twenty-four-foot trailer during a rainstorm along the winding roads of the Oregon Coast, wedged between a mountain cliff and drop-off down to the ocean. The common thread was adventure and spending time together as a family.

It was on an excursion to Saskatoon, where my Dad's parents, Granddad Hal and Grandma Lil, lived, that I first experienced shooting a live animal—in this case, a gopher. These pesky diggers give local farmers hell. Gophers dig holes everywhere, each one a potential death trap for a cow. If a cow steps into a hole and breaks a leg, which is likely, the farmer has to shoot it to put it out of its misery. And there goes a part of that family's livelihood, not to mention the premature death of a cow. Granddad Hal, Dad, and Bran were charged with getting rid of as many gophers as they could.

Imagine Dad's surprise when he asked if I wanted to go with the boys and I said yes.

Before we walked out to the field where cows grazed in rolling green pastures, I saw Mom pull Dad aside. She looked concerned. I overheard her whisper, "Don't force her, Jim. Don't pressure her into anything."

Dad nodded. Point taken.

The four of us headed out toward the field, me sandwiched among three generations of men (well, one a boy). As I walked, I kept rolling up the too-long sleeves of Bran's jacket. "It's so cool you're coming," he said. "The farmer gives us twenty-five cents for every gopher we bring back!"

As the guys set up our site on a hill, I was reeling with excitement. The field below looked like a canvas of polka dots—gopher holes dug across every few feet of ground.

Bran lay down, propped his air gun on Dad's backpack, and took his first shot. All of a sudden, gopher mania broke loose. A swarm of small brown creatures scurried around, attempting to dive to safety. When the dust cleared, we saw that my brother had hit his mark, earning his first quarter that day.

Now I wanted a turn. "Dad," I piped up, "I wanna try."

Without giving me time to think twice, my dad reloaded the air gun and laid it back down on the backpack, waiting for me to take position. "It's just like a target, Eve," he said calmly. "Just like a target."

But was it? Shooting a live animal is much different from shooting at a target. When you're aiming at an empty aluminum can or at an orange bullseye stapled to a fence post, there's nothing at stake. But when you've got wildlife in your line of sight, your adrenaline shoots through the roof. You start breathing faster. Your heart feels as if it's going to jump out of your chest. The goal is to get calm and stay steady.

I spotted a gopher just under thirty yards away. "Wait until he stands still," Dad said, pausing for me to reposition the crosshairs. "Now, if you're ready, squeeze the trigger. Slowly. Just like with a target."

As I'd been taught, I exhaled. And in slow motion, pulling back my pointer finger on the cool metal, I took the shot.

Caught in a pulse-pounding adrenaline rush, I gasped when I saw the animal go down. But Dad looked disappointed. "It's okay, Eve. You missed it," he said.

Huh?

"Don't worry," Dad said, grabbing the gun to reload it. "You'll find another one."

I squinted out toward the field. "No, Dad, I hit it. I saw him go down."

He didn't seem convinced. "Okay, let's go check."

After we made the short trek down the hill, Dad stopped about ten yards short of the gopher I'd aimed at. "See?" he said, looking around. "He's gone."

Confused, I continued walking a bit farther until I found a gopher lying motionless next to a hole. This was the one that I'd had in my sights. "See, Dad? He's right here."

When he realized what had happened, Dad roared. "Holy moly, Eve! You just got your first gopher! We must've been looking at two different gophers when you shot!" For the next few minutes, he kept repeating "Holy moly" and "Holy smokes" over and over and over again.

I couldn't stop smiling. Not only did I earn a quarter, I learned something that day: I could hang with the boys. I could be a full participant and make my own contribution. For the first time, I felt fully tied in to this part of our family dynamic, a tapestry of values, respect, and togetherness. It was a natural feeling, a good feeling. Oh, I had much to learn about the hunting lifestyle, and many years passed before I did. But that day, I felt accomplished. Looking back, I'd even say it was a turning point.

I had done something no one had thought I would.

2

"JUST GIVE IT A CHANCE"

A journey of a thousand miles begins with a single step.

—LAO TZU

TANZANIA, EAST AFRICA, 2002

I didn't want to go.

I dragged my empty duffle bag out from under the bunk and started tossing in shorts and tanks and flip-flops. Sitting on the edge of the bed, my summer-camp friends attempted feebly to console me.

"You're going to have so much fun," one said while lacing up her hiking boots.

Beach towel in hand, another girl started piling on sunscreen. "Going to Africa would be so cool. I wish I was going!"

I smiled, trying to appreciate their kind though pitying words. Not wanting to come across as a brat because I didn't want to go to Tanzania with my family, I responded half-heartedly, "Aw, guys. You're all just saying that because you get to stay here at camp."

When Mom and Dad shared the news that summer camp would be cut short because we were spending a month in Africa on one of Dad's trips, I'd whined in typical teenage fashion. Eye rolls, theatric inflections, the works. Ignoring my pout-fest, my parents were firm in their reply: "There's more to life than this little bubble you live in, Eve."

I was a fourteen-year-old girl, navigating garden-variety teenage mood swings that drove me from being as cheery as pie one minute to a drama queen the next. The last thing I wanted to do was spend a month with my parents and brother in the bush. I wanted to stay at summer camp with my friends. I wanted to boat and tube and float and get a suntan. Hanging out with my family on a hunting trip was nowhere near my radar. Especially when it was going to be recorded on camera for the world to see.

By this time in 2002, Dad was filming his TV show, *Jim Shockey's Hunting Adventures*. Airing only in the States at that point, it highlighted his hunting escapades all over the world. So while having a twenty-pound old-school video camera slung in our direction 24/7 wasn't a new occurrence on our family trips, it still wasn't something I enjoyed. I didn't want a camera in my face highlighting my sourpuss expression or a forced smile for all eternity. But, hey, what choice did I have?

On a sunny August afternoon, we all walked onto the first of four flights that would bring us deep into the African continent. Final destination: a hunting camp in the swamps that are part of the Moyowosi Game Reserve, Tanzania, East Africa. Our final charter plane landed near camp, where the runway was nothing more than a dirt path marked by potholes and random tufts of grass.

Through the smudged Plexiglas window, I could see the PH (Professional Hunter) waving at us. The owner of the hunting company, he was in charge of guiding us throughout our stay on safari and leading Dad on his hunts. Beside him stood a handful of smiling African trackers, locals who could spot and track animals with remarkable precision. As presentable as they all looked, their clothing was caked with a thin layer of dust—one of the "perks," I would soon learn, of spending all day in the bush.

I debarked in a haze. Noticing my discomfort, Mom offered, "Honey, just take a deep breath, and take it all in. It's good for us to get out of our comfort zones."

I groaned. "I stepped out of my comfort zone the minute I stepped off the plane, Mom. It's so hot here. And probably no one even speaks English."

Mom smiled, trying to be sympathetic. "Just give it a chance."

As Dad carried on with the PH as if they were long-lost friends, we climbed into a Land Rover and took off for the camp. Another bumpy journey led us deep into the swamps, the wetlands of the northeastern part of the country, where a network of marshes, acacia woodlands, and rolling grassy plains create ideal conditions for hunting large game. Zebra, buffalo, wildebeest, warthogs, and topi roam the open spaces, while in the swamplands, gargantuan hippos and deadly crocodiles command the top of the food chain.

Here's the thing. I didn't go to Africa expecting to stay at a five-star resort. Still, I was a bit shocked to see how rustic camp was. Situated on an open plain dotted with pockets of dry grass and acacia trees, their branches spread out gracefully like an umbrella canopy, our "cabins" were nothing more than tented space underneath traditional thatched roofs.

Before we settled into our tents, the PH offered a warning. "We've had a lot of wildlife coming through camp lately, especially at night. Hyena tracks everywhere. Even had an aggressive male lion come right into camp and do some damage. I had no choice but to shoot him."

My eyes grew wide as he continued. "During the day, you can walk around as you please, but keep an eye on your surroundings. Never let your guard down. And at night, stay in your tents. These animals can hide in the thick grasses, so it's best to stay inside. If you see anything unusual, just start yelling." He pointed to a similar-looking tented space a few yards away. "We're not far away." Well, that speech got my adrenaline rushing—in part from the spine-tingling thought that a predator could be lurking right outside my tent, but also because it was pretty cool to think I might get to see a hyena or a lion in real life.

When Dad and Bran took off with the PH and the trackers early in the mornings for their long days of hunting, I stayed behind with Mom. Though I kept to my grumpy self, I couldn't help but marvel at the locals who worked at the lodge. They whipped up extraordinary meals in the absence of a stove, microwave, or fridge. And they were always happy, singing and laughing the day away.

Still, I was determined to prove how unhappy I was that my parents had dragged me away from summer camp. (Like I said, typical teenager.)

Mom tried to intervene. "Eva, come take a walk with me," she'd say one day, camera slung around her neck.

"No thanks," I'd reply, curled up in my mosquito-netted cot, wondering what my friends were doing back home. *Why am I here? I'm so bored.*

Whipping out her mat, she'd ask the next day, "Eva, how about doing some yoga with me?"

"No thanks."

For at least a few days, I was stuck on being miserable. Coupled with missing summer camp, friends, and fun, I was hot, covered in dirt, and constantly getting bitten by swarms of tsetse flies. The more I focused on these things, the further I slipped into an emotional no-man's land.

That is, until Mom made me laugh.

A yoga instructor by then, Mom practiced her craft all the time. One day, as I lay in my favorite place, bed, reading a teen magazine, she started showing off her flexibility. "Hey, Eve, look what I can do!" she exclaimed while bending the top half of her body parallel to the floor and then threading each arm under an outstretched leg.

Without a lick of emotion, I replied, "That's awesome, Mom." My eyes rolled from my magazine to Mom's contorted body.

I heard her grunt softly as her body rustled around in that weird position. Then the grunt got louder and the rustling more intense. Finally, an alarming gasp. "Eve, I'm stuck!" With a desperate look on her face, Mom started to giggle. "No guff. I can't move!"

"C'mon, Mom, just stop," I said, trying hard not to smile.

"Eve, I'm not joking. I seriously need help," she said. More grunting and gasping.

And then, I just couldn't help it. I burst out laughing. So did Mom. In that moment, my façade of gloom shattered. All the wonder that I had been holding hostage was suddenly released. After helping Mom untangle her body from the dreadful pose, I started gushing about what I had been too stubborn to admit before. "Mom! This place is actually pretty cool! I can't believe there was a fresh lion track outside our tent this morning. And the zebra stew last night for dinner was amazing! And everyone here is so happy!"

I realized something important on that trip. Even though we lived in different parts of the world and held different cultural and religious beliefs, the staff, many of them local villagers, and the Shockeys were the same—human beings created by God. The people we met at camp were family oriented, too. They provided for their children and loved to have fun—just like us. Oh, sure, they may have worn loincloths instead of khakis, but we shared many things in common.

It's funny what happens when you're forced to stretch your awareness beyond your comfort zone. My parents didn't travel because we had a bunch of extra money lying around. Mom and Dad chose to scrimp and save and even double mortgage their house in order to take those trips, but they did it so Bran and I could explore other cultures, customs, and ways of life. They wanted us to understand that, yes, the world was, in fact, a lot bigger than the one we knew. They also knew that being together as a family and being involved in Dad's world would leave lasting imprints on our character and on who we would one day become.

› › ›

By the time I got to high school and began contemplating the future, it made sense to expect that I would go away to university. But I still didn't know what I wanted to do when I grew up. Dance remained all-consuming for me. I was in the studio seven days a week, but midway through high school, I realized that I didn't actually want to make a career out of it. The early-morning practices and nonstop competition were beginning to wear on me. Not to mention all the practices and games I had all throughout high school for tennis and field hockey. I had to consider other options.

In the tenth grade, roaming the cubicles of a college fair, I stumbled into a presentation for Bond University, a college on the Gold Coast of Australia. The school offered a fully accredited degree in business marketing with a minor in events management. This accelerated program would allow me to finish my education in two years. While Australia was a far 7,300 miles away from home, I was beginning to recognize my need for adventure.

In fact, the summer before, I'd chosen to study abroad in Spain, where I took some classes and worked as a nanny.

I also enjoyed my first taste of independence. I lived in a Gothic-style convent in Salamanca. I learned the art of bull-fighting in Toledo with a red cape and a fuming bull, and I became practically fluent in Spanish. It was amazing to see the rewards from pushing myself out of the cozy family nest and into the unknown. I learned so much, I spent each summer thereafter working and studying abroad until I finished high school.

When it finally came time to leave for university, I remember standing in my bedroom closet, gazing at my dance costumes hanging on cushioned hangers, a mélange of shiny fabrics and sequins at rest. Slowly, I tied the silky ribbons of my ballet slippers into a knot and hung them on a hook on the wall. I stared at them for a while, wondering if I'd ever wear them again.

Thinking it would be a great idea to start my college adventure alone, I turned down my parents' offer to fly to Australia with me and help me get settled. So on January 4, 2007, the day before my nineteenth birthday (the Canadian equivalent of a twenty-first birthday in the States), I flew from British Columbia to Australia, seventeen hours ahead in time difference. I touched down in the "Land Down Under" on the sixth. It was as if my birthday on the fifth never happened. Suddenly alone, I felt punched in the gut by homesickness.

But quickly I forged a new life on the other side of the world. While much of it was positive, some of the good habits I had formed over the years started losing their grip on me. Without dance and sports, I wasn't physically active.

And in the absence of healthy meals, I was introduced to such college-student delicacies as instant ramen noodles and boxed mac and cheese. I remember going to a grocery store for the first time in my life. Having never eaten any meat but wild game, I spent twenty minutes interrogating the butcher about the options. Let's just say my first attempt at cooking was a bust. And, nothing against supermarket meat, but once you've eaten organic and free-range wild game, nothing else will do. Since I couldn't replicate Mom's recipes, I opted for easy. If a food item could be prepared with minimal to zero effort and tasted delicious, I was sold. It didn't take long to add twenty pounds to my five-foot-six frame. I didn't body-shame myself, but I did miss feeling strong and fit.

I graduated in early 2009 with my bachelor's degree and the goal of becoming an event planner. The blueprint I'd mapped out for my immediate future was simple: fly home and attend a hunting expo with my family, apply for a work visa, then go back to Australia to look for a job. Though I had talked to my parents regularly and had seen them for short visits, I was long overdue for some serious family time.

I arrived on Vancouver Island in the beginning of 2009, just in time for trade-show season. In January of every year since I can remember, our family has attended a number of hunting expos and conferences, big ones that boast crowds in the thousands. It was always neat to get a glimpse into Dad's world and notice the ripples he was making in the outdoor industry. But while this was roughly my twentieth trade show, something felt different this time around.

The convention center was packed with ten-thousand-plus

men and the odd woman who loved to hunt, fish, and explore the great outdoors. I noticed the warmth in their manner-isms, their wide smiles, the way their eyes lit up when they discovered a new product or met someone who wanted to swap hunting stories. They loved conservation. They loved to travel. They loved adventure. And it didn't matter how exotic or familiar the experience, whether it was camping in their own backyard or hunting brown bears in Alaska, this was a passionate bunch.

I walked around the venue, weaving slowly up and down the seven-plus miles of rows, brushing elbows with thousands of fellow visitors. I was mesmerized by the countless booths showcasing the latest hunting gear, taxidermy, and artwork from around the world, as well as the many opportunities to book hunts and chat with industry professionals who were more than willing to divulge tips and share experiences. In passing, I caught bits and pieces of conversations.

"An African safari has been on my bucket list for years. Let's go over to that booth and find out more."

"I want to bring my son on a hunt he'll never forget for his graduation present."

"Did you see that world-record moose mount by the en-trance? I've never seen antlers that big!"

As I'd often done, I watched Dad from the sidelines. Lis-tening to him captivate audiences at banquets and seminars with his stories and knowledge, it was almost like being in-troduced to my father for the first time. I saw him in a dif-ferent light, as a true pioneer in his field. Though I'd always known him to be raw and real, that day I was reminded that, no matter how many hunting awards he won or records he broke (and these were plentiful as the years went on), his passion for hunting itself was always front and center for him.

As I took in the sights and sounds of old friends reuniting and sharing memories, strangers getting acquainted and making plans to build new memories, my heart pounded. Maybe the future I had mapped out for myself wasn't the right one. Maybe there was more to life than planning events for others. I sensed possibility calling, a new door opening. And with the whisper of the great unknown gnawing at my spirit, I had a change of heart. I realized I didn't want to go back to Australia. I wanted to stay in North America. For the first time, I wanted to figure out why my dad cared so much about what he did for a living. More important, I wanted to know if I could share that enthusiasm and find a place in his world. To do that, I'd need to have the full experience.

I'll never forget walking into Dad's office a few days after that trade show. Sitting in front of his bulky, early-edition laptop, he pounded away with fury, the clacking keys echoing throughout his taxidermy-filled man cave. Hundreds of African artifacts cluttered shelves and display cases. I plopped down in the swivel chair in front of his antique writing desk, noticing the glass eyes of many antlered animals gazing down at me from the walls. After doing a spin or two in my chair, with Dad's eyes still glued to his screen, I casually announced, "Dad, I want to learn how to hunt."

The clacking of the keys stopped. Dad looked up, and his jaw dropped in dramatic cartoon fashion. I could tell he was waiting for me to add, "Just kidding!"

But I didn't.

So he looked at me, eyes as wide as saucers, and asked, "Why?"

"I want to see and understand exactly what you do. I want to know why you love it so much."

No doubt about it, Dad was thrilled. A big smile panned over his face. But after a minute of beaming, he wasted no time giving me a reality check. "You need to know what you're getting into, Eve. If you're going to do this, you are going to come across a lot of people who won't like you because of it."

Dad leaned forward in his chair, his brow furrowed. "Critics and anti-hunters are going to pop up left and right. They're going to say mean, nasty things about you. And people from extremist animal-rights groups might even get violent. They might follow you, find out where you live, and stalk you. You could even get a bomb in the mail. Trust me, Eve, I've had a ton of experience with extremist groups. I had eighty-eight death threats in one day alone!"

I nodded, taking note of Dad's counsel. I remembered as a kid seeing Mom freak out about an envelope that had come for Dad in the mail. I found out later it contained razor blades covered with poison. Unlike in today's world of social media, where people hurl insults via computer or phone screens, back in the day, the haters used the telephone or snail mail. Or firebombs. My dad knew an outfitter who had discovered—fortunately, just in a time—a bomb on his boat. It had been planted there by an animal-rights group. A number of organizations did then and still do incite violent acts against people and property in the name of liberating animals from the tyranny of humans. One group in particular was even named a terrorist threat by the U.S. government in 2005.

"Sure, Dad," I responded, "I know." Oh, his words were somewhat frightening, but I didn't really understand them at the time. I didn't have the experience to fully appreciate the warning. And all I knew in that moment was that I wanted to hunt.

My father continued the heart-to-heart. "You're an easy target, Eve. You're young. You're a female. You come from a family of hunters. People are going to try to convince you that what you're doing is wrong. And in the process they are going to say a lot of harsh things."

"I'll be fine, Dad. I won't let it bother me," I said with a reassuring smile.

Turns out, hunting requires a lot more paperwork and to-do lists than I'd imagined. I had to get a gun permit and a hunting license, which meant taking courses and classes and learning about things that make total sense but that I'd never given much thought to. And, equally important, I'd have to schedule a trip. Not to mention, considering my decision to stay home in North America, I'd also need to figure out a way to pay my bills. I found a full-time job in the city of Vancouver, a few hours away, and started teaching Latin salsa classes five days a week. Reuniting with dance was a way of getting in shape, since, well, I wasn't. I was tired of feeling tired, sluggish, and weak. I wanted my groove back.

When Mom first found out about my decision to hunt,

she was shocked. "Wow! This isn't something I ever thought I'd hear. Are you sure you want to do this? I mean, once you shoot a big game animal, you can't take it back, Eva. People will label you a hunter forever. Are you ready for that?" Mom was, perhaps, a bit afraid that she was losing her "little dancer," aficionado of all things girly, to the man's world of hunting.

Fortunately, she realized quickly what mattered most. She knew I'd need her support a lot more than I knew at the time. I didn't know a single woman hunter I could lean on for advice. While Mom understood the lifestyle only as an observer, she became a necessary ally, especially when my close friends thought I was losing my mind.

Mom went above and beyond in support of my decision. "Let me take the hunting course with you," she offered. I gladly accepted. For seven hours straight for three days, Mom sat with me in a room with about ten other people, some old, some young, all male, learning the basic rules and regulations of hunting. The instructor spent more time than I thought possible talking about how to identify animals by their tracks, which animals can be hunted and when, and the proper use of firearms and bows. Talk about information overload. Never mind feeling like a black swan in a class full of middle-aged white men with a few male teenagers speckling the group, I'd never before felt so uneducated. As I sat at a desk listening to the instructor drone on and on about federal gun laws, different types of ammunition, and the inner workings of firearms as they progressed from the first gun invented in the thirteenth century until today, I was overwhelmed. My brain was about to explode.

Then came talk of conservation. My ears perked up. To me, conservation seemed a bit alien in a hunting course. I'd always assumed hunting was as simple as going somewhere in the woods and killing whatever, whenever, however. But there's science behind it: ecology. Scientists the world over regularly assess wildlife populations, the land that supports them, the amount of crop damage the animals might do, and the extent of disease outbreaks among herds. This determines what and how many animals hunters can harvest without endangering an area's wildlife population. Not only that, but thanks to the Pittman-Robertson Act passed in 1937, a tax imposed on the sale of firearms and ammunition in the United States is distributed by the government to game and fish agencies across the country to help restore and manage wildlife habitats. This legislation generates $700 million annually to help preserve wildlife. Yet another way hunters are conservationists! And if hunters don't thin the population of certain animals, those same animals would not survive in their environments as more and more land is developed for human use, which consequently decreases the amount of available vegetation for animals to consume.

The more I understood the facts about the positive impact hunters make, the more a heartfelt desire to hunt began to open up in me. This made the difference between simply being okay with others hunting versus wanting to do it myself.

I passed the hunting course and started working to earn my gun permit. Once I could legally lock and load, I hit the range often with my dad for target practice. Usually the only female in a crowd of gun enthusiasts, police officers, and hunters, I aimed at the paper targets placed at the fifty-, one-hundred-, and two-hundred-yard marks, with Dad yelling repeatedly through my protective earmuffs, "Just squeeze the trigger slowly. Don't jerk your finger. Focus on the target, and squeeze." It was weird to think that, in a few months, there'd be a live big-game animal in my sights. I'd be responsible for making a good, clean shot. I'd have to execute under pressure.

You can understand the rules of how to handle and shoot a firearm. You can go to the range and hit the center ring of a bullseye a million times. But nothing can prepare you for the moment when it's time to pull the trigger on a live big animal.

> 3 ‹

TAKING AIM

The comfort zone is a great enemy of the human potential.[1]
—BRIAN TRACY

SOUTH AFRICA, 2009
››

It's a mob scene.

One minute I'm reclining on a quiet European jet full of napping and movie-watching passengers. The next I'm hurried into a chaotic space of sensory overload, reeling with the onslaught of movement and sound. Hundreds of locals flood the Johannesburg, South Africa, airport, their voices loud but mostly incomprehensible to me—African languages scattered with a few recognizable English words. Sweat drips down my temples and the inside of my shirt. As I clutch the handle of my carry-on suitcase, Dad warns, "Stay close." I sidle up to Mom as she grabs my father's hand tightly.

"Taxi?" A young man flashing a megawatt smile appears inches away from my face. I stare at him with eyes wide. "Taxi? Taxi?" he repeats as if I'm hard of hearing. Not waiting for my reply, the man reaches for my bag, his other hand waving wildly in my face, signaling me to come with him. His breath is hot and far too close for comfort. Dad squeezes quickly between me and the stranger. He puts the palm of his hand a few inches away from the man's face and couples this with an intimidating glare. We may be tourists in this foreign land, but Dad knows what he's doing. He's not being mean; he's being vigilant. Johannesburg, South Africa, was and still is one of the most dangerous cities in the world.

The process of collecting our gun cases and suitcases full of hunting gear goes by in a blur. Everything seems to occur in triple time—with so much commotion, I can hardly keep up.

"Passports!" a stoic-faced airport person demands.

Another commands, "Permits!"

Our papers are pored over with intense scrutiny. Luggage, boxes of gear, and gun cases are rummaged through with quick hands. The rapid-fire verbal interactions are intimidating. I shuffle, shell-shocked, from one customs officer to another, from one inspection room to another, from this counter to that one to pay for our gun permits and whatever else local officials claim is a fee that we owe them. Then, just after midnight, we're on our way to the hotel, where we will try to catch a few hours of sleep.

This is it. My first hunt.

The next morning, another flight and two hours of traveling by Jeep bring us to the hunting lodge in Port Elizabeth. Russ, our boyish-looking PH, greets us warmly. "Welcome to paradise," he says. His South African accent is thick, his cheeriness contagious. He and his colleagues collect our bags.

With wide eyes I explore where I will spend the next three weeks. The vanilla stucco hunting lodge looks tiny in the middle of an open plain that unfolds in a carpet of velvet green. Mountains tower around the property in the distance. It reminds me of what Baroness Karen Blixen wrote about the African land in her memoir *Out of Africa*: "The views were immensely wide. Everything that you saw made for greatness and freedom, and unequalled nobility."[2]

The first item on our agenda on day two, prior to my hunting adventure? Photo safari.

"Keep your eyes open," the PH calls out as Mom and I stand in the bed of a safari Jeep. Our knuckles are white from our death grip on a handlebar of sorts. Binoculars in hand, Dad's planted like a tree, comfortable, in his element. Tires churn swiftly on the off-road path, splattering us with dust that swirls in giant clouds. Watching *National Geographic* or high-definition imagery online is nothing like your own eyes soaking up the sights and sounds of the African wild.

"Look into the bush for movement," Russ reminds us. "Right over there! Look! Look!"

A herd of lanky giraffes moves toward an Acacia tree. The first in line arches her neck to munch on the topmost leaves. I notice that the two who lag behind move both legs on one side of their bodies in unison, then the other pair on the other side, a walk unique to the giraffe. The hours move fast along this trail of wonder and awe. Nimble springbok, the South African national animal, graze in the thinly grassed plains. An arc of leaping impala, elegant and quick, move seamlessly in a wave, their red and white bodies in sync. Hours later, I almost have a heart attack when an adult elephant, ears flapping, starts to charge, his six-ton body rushing toward us in an uncanny cadence of speed and agility. I finally exhale when he stops just thirty yards shy of our vehicle. Watching the wild unfold before my eyes reminds me of why I'm on African soil. I'm here not just to gape at the beauty of the bush. I'm also here to hunt.

A day or two after going on safari, I sit with Dad in the main lodge, a room oozing warmth with its stone fireplace, high wood-beamed ceilings, deep red and orange upholstery, and striking African statues. Scores of animal mounts dot the walls: spiral-horned nyalas, springbok, fawn-colored hartebeests, and warthogs with scary-looking tusks projecting out of their mouths.

Sitting close together on a chocolate leather couch that's draped with a hide of some sort, we decide that the warthog will be the first animal I will hunt. Members of the pig family, warthogs don't win any prizes in the beauty department—a major plus, since I'm not sure I'll be able to pull the trigger on a majestic or cute and cuddly animal with long, sweetly batting eyelashes. Coarse hair in random patches adorns a warthog's barrel-shaped body. Its shovel-shaped head showcases huge wartlike bumps, pockets of fat that help protect it from predators. What look like long tusks on its face are actually teeth. With them, the animals cause a lot of agricultural damage, bedeviling local farmers. But Dad's reason for hunting warthog is purely logical. "They're good to eat," he says. This is important, because it's customary for us to eat some of the meat ourselves and donate the rest to feed the staff at the hunting lodge, as well as the local villagers. "You can stalk them pretty easily. A perfect animal for the beginner hunter," he concludes with a smile, clapping me on the back.

Eager to flaunt my knowledge of African animals, I grab a photo album from a nearby table and spread it across my lap. Every picture features a hunter who came to the area and the animal he hunted. Back home, I'd read books, watched documentaries, and spent countless hours online learning about the different species of African wild game. I was confident I could apply that knowledge effortlessly in the bush. It was time to show off.

"Okay, Dad. Let's go. Test me."

Dad points to one glossy four-by-six and asks, "What animal is this?"

I stare at the photograph but draw a blank. "A kudu?"

Dad smiles and shakes his head. "Nope, it's a nyala. See that white chevron between his eyes? Okay, let's keep going."

We do this for an hour. Suffice it to say, I can only name—and I'm probably being generous—one out of every ten animals Dad points to. As he continues to ask me questions and I continue replying with the wrong answer, Dad chuckles. I laugh halfheartedly. *Holy smokes, I can't even name an animal in a photograph; how on earth am I supposed to hunt one?* The confidence I acquired back home starts to fade. *What am I doing here?*

I know that no one is expecting me to recognize every South African animal by its looks, how it jumps or runs, or how long its horns are. But I don't want to show up to the hunt without knowing the name of the animal standing in front of me. Sitting on that dark leather couch with Dad, I feel unprepared.

I remember vividly the few weeks before the trip, when I was trying to figure out what to pack. As the spokesperson for a company that made functional and fashionable outdoor clothing for women, Mom had an arsenal of safari wear. Sweeping her hand over the bombardment of button-down shirts, cargo pants, brush pants, vests, and jackets laid out on her bed, she said, "Dive in, sweetie!" Of course, squeezing into clothes meant for my five-foot-eight, 110-pound-soaking-wet mother while still carrying my extra weight from university wasn't an ideal way to boost my confidence for the upcoming trip.

Rummaging through the articles of olive and khaki cotton clothing, I held up a pair of pants. *Sigh.* I'd never be able to button them over my burgeoning middle.

Mom noticed my expression and nodded sympathetically. "How about these?" she asked, offering another pair with an elastic waistband.

"Not even close," I said, my cheeks tinged with red.

Besides the fact that I'd had to order clothes in a bigger size than I'd ever worn (and then place another order because that first batch was still too small), I wasn't totally sure what to bring. Mom was helpful to a degree, but only to the extent of what I'd need for camp, not the actual hunt. And Dad? He, too, provided somewhat valuable information. I'm sure he assumed I could figure it out on my own, using common sense. If so, boy, was he wrong.

I thought my logic was sound for packing a million pairs

of shorts. It's Africa. It's hot. Shorts are meant for hot weather. Wrong! Shorts don't work when you're crawling up a rocky path or pushing through sharp weeds and thorny bushes. I also didn't realize that wearing two pairs of socks at a time would help prevent blisters or that baby wipes would be a blessing, especially because I wouldn't be able to buy them once we touched down in Africa, and that a hat to protect against the blazing sun was a must, not to mention binoculars, which to this day I'm still not sure whether or not I packed. In hindsight, many of the items in my duffle bag weren't the most appropriate. I would learn firsthand during the trip what was.

› › ›

The sky on hunting day fans out in brilliant colors. Nerves and excitement spar as I bump along an unpaved road with my parents, three or four trackers, and Russ. Our vehicle kicks up a dust storm, sprinkling my sweat-sticky skin and hair with a thin coat of dirt. We finally get to the drop-off point. Warthog haven is inaccessible by vehicle and lies a couple of hours away on foot. Not wanting to spook other animals nearby, we get out of the vehicle slowly and quietly. Dad preps the muzzleloader, the heavy firearm I'll use for the hunt.

Every hunter prefers a certain weapon, based on the wild game they are hunting, how far away they are shooting, and so on. Some prefer using a compound bow. I use a bow on some of the hunts you'll read about, so bear with me while I explain, for those who don't know what it is. Unlike a simple recurve (stick and string) bow, a compound bow is a complex system of cams, cables, pulleys, and other gizmos designed to maximize power, speed, and accuracy. This type of bow is engineered to pull back the peak weight of the draw ("draw weight") and then "let off" when the bow is in full draw. Once this happens, you're pulling back only a percentage of the draw weight, which makes it easier to hold the bow in position longer. A compound bow is also designed to draw back and stop at a certain point, based on your arm span, known as the draw length. Using a bow is more challenging than a gun, so I make sure I have put in a lot of practice hours shooting my bow before I use it to hunt.

Some hunters prefer using a rifle, others a shotgun. The list is long. While I use a rifle now and prefer it, I started out using a muzzleloader. Delivering only a single shot per load, this traditional firearm is a pretty challenging weapon of choice.

"Walk quietly, Eve," Dad whispers from behind me as we enter the bush, mere miles away from jagged, rocky cliffs overlooking the sparkling Indian Ocean. As we step softly through shrubby, thorny bushveld and rolling hills punctuated by aloe bushes and euphorbia trees that ooze white milky sap, my leg muscles start to burn. Mom and the men trek with relative ease. Sweating and panting with every stride, I try not to fall behind.

Two or three hours of hiking bring us to the moment of truth: seventy-five yards away is a napping, mature, male warthog. A tracker signals discreetly with a quiet whistle, pointing at the animal.

"Big pig. Sleeping," Dad whispers of the boar.

Be still, my beating heart.

Russ, shooting sticks in hand, digs the three-legged, rubber-clawed base into the dirt and adjusts the height to shoulder level. Dad pulls the primer from his pocket and drops it into place within my muzzleloader.

I stand behind Russ, trying to steady my quivering hands. A fundamental rule of hunting is to stay calm. It's amazing how hard that can be when the pressure is on.

"Get into position, Eve. He'll probably get up any second now," Dad offers as I try to lull my quick and heavy breaths.

I mount the muzzleloader into the V-shaped yoke. *Inhale. Exhale. Repeat.* Dad continues to whisper in my ear, guiding my every move. I listen to every word, learning with each bit of instruction.

"It's just like shooting at a target. When he gets up, make sure you're solid on him. When you know you're aimed at the right spot, slowly squeeze the trigger."

I nod, turning back with a nervous smile. Ah, the right spot. I had almost forgotten about that important piece of information. The vital organs of African animals are placed more forward in the chest than those of North American animals. A number of international hunters who hunt in Africa don't know this and end up wounding an animal on the first shot because they aim too far back. Dad and I had carefully reviewed where on the body to aim at certain animals in this part of the world, but the minute the warthog stands up, glaring at me for interrupting his siesta, the knowledge flies out the window.

As the calmness I had just nursed vanishes and my heart regains its erratic rhythm, pressure digs into my bones. *Hurry up and pull the trigger,* my inner voice screams, but it's essential to make a good shot, and you won't do that if you feel rushed. I remember Dad telling me over and over to approach a hunt as if I have only one bullet. "Make the shot count," he would tell me. "If you think that you have extra bullets to use, you won't put your full focus into your first shot." But with the type of gun I'm using, I have no choice but to approach it that way. I really do have just one shot.

Teetering on the brink of hyperventilating, I have to wait. Take long, deep breaths. Steady my mind. Steady my heart. Steady my hands.

"Get ready, get ready," Dad repeats.

I start inching my way back to inner center. "Do I shoot him now?"

"No, wait."

"So when do I shoot him?"

"You just have to wait."

Not being the most patient person in the universe, I find this waiting bit annoying.

"Take him just under the tusk," Dad instructs, guiding my aim to the hog's vitals.

I steady the muzzleloader and set the crosshairs on—wait, which tusk? "The left one?" I ask.

"Yes. Aim about three inches below his left tusk."

I cock the hammer and slowly squeeze the trigger. My ears get blasted by the echoing shot. I squint through the cloud of smoke that spits out of the barrel. *Where did he go?*

"Did I miss him?"

"No, Eve, you got him." Dad had heard the thud of the bullet penetrating the hog's chest.

"I'm about to cry," I say, as my lip trembles and my hands shake. A tear slides down my cheek. Dad hugs me, proud. Mom, who had been standing back taking pictures, now puts an arm around me. Enveloped by parental love and paralyzing shock in one of the most emotion-ridden moments in my life, I cry. The buildup to this moment—the hours spent in a classroom learning the basics of hunting, in target practice, in trying to figure out what to wear, what to pack, wondering what it would feel like with an animal in my crosshairs, wrenched with the fear of the unknown—all of it bubbles to the surface. I break down. It's not tears of sadness that cascade down my sunburned cheeks. It's a release. A flood of weight seems to tumble off my body.

I did it. And I want to do it again.

Later, I watch the men carry the warthog to the skinning shed in camp. Using a pulley system, they hoist it up by its two hind legs. Once the warthog is stretched out taut, ready to be skinned and gutted, the animal's hide is peeled back by expert hands. Precautions are taken not to contaminate the meat as quarters are sliced and organs and intestines tossed into nearby buckets for the villagers to use for various purposes. I'm not repulsed by the gore as a rush of blood spills out of the hog's abdominal cavity and splatters the concrete floor. My memory takes me back to that skinned moose hanging in our carport when I was a kid. I'd thought it was pretty gross, dirty, retch-worthy, sure. But this day, having hunted the animal myself to serve as food for us and for the locals, I feel connected to the process in a way I hadn't known was possible.

When the gutting and quartering is over, I stand face-to-face with a carcass of warthog bones. It's a spiritual moment. This animal had given its life for us. And when I sit down to dinner that night and feast on tender hog chops cooked in a mouthwatering stew laden with herbs and spices, I can't help but feel proud. I'm eating something I harvested on my own. Call it "field to table."

> › › ›

Before that life-changing trip's end, I went on two more hunts, harvesting a black wildebeest and an impala. I left South Africa nursing a slightly burned scalp from not wearing a hat and a couple of blisters on my aching feet. But, physical nuisances aside, my spirit was settled. I knew beyond a shadow of a doubt that my life as just an observer in Dad's hunting world was over.

I arrived back in Vancouver eager to learn more about hunting, to explore wildlife, and to research conservation programs. I wanted to pick Dad's brain and his boundless wealth of knowledge. I wanted to buy sturdier hiking boots. I wanted to get in better shape so I could hike mountains with ease. I wanted to join the local archery club. I wanted to practice shooting with a compound bow (I had brought my first one ever and started practicing with it on the trip) and with a gun. More than anything, I wanted to go on another hunt. And I didn't want to waste any time getting started.

Of course, it wasn't as if I could go on an immediate hunting binge. I had to figure out how to weave my newfound passion into my current job as a nanny and dance teacher.

The day after I got back from Africa, I ate dinner with my friends from salsa class. We'd often grab a bite to eat after class and later go dancing at the clubs. About ten of us rounded the table that day, talking loudly, our conversation blending English and Spanish. As baskets of tortilla chips and fresh guacamole were passed, uptempo and passion-laden music trumpeted in the background.

It had been three weeks since I'd left this fast-paced city life of working all day, dancing all night, and waking up to do it all again. But as much as I appreciated the conveniences of living downtown, a part of me now felt empty. I missed the glorious sunrises over the African plains, the fierce and gentle movements of the wild, the feeling of my pounding heartbeat as I looked at an animal in the crosshairs of my gun.

Someone at the table asked, "So, how was your trip, Eva?"

"Awesome!" I said. And with much gusto and in full color I relayed my experience on safari. Then, with equal excitement, I blurted, "And then we went on several hunts!"

With that last word, time seemed to stop. Even the tune blaring from the speakers seemed to screech to a halt. All eyes were fixed on me.

"Did *you* hunt?" one guy asked, not even attempting to hide the judgment in his voice.

"Yeah, I did."

The head honcho of the dance school, a man with a bold personality, quick to offer whatever was on his mind, appropriate or not, said, "I can't believe you shot something. That's so weird." He started cracking up, looking around the table for fellow dancers to support his opinion. A few did, chuckling in both hilarity and horror. One guy pretended to be a sad animal, crying, as he gestured to mimic being shot. Another chimed in, "You are so mean, Eva! Those poor animals!" Someone else said, "I would never kill a helpless animal!" Most around the table seemed to agree.

I was at a loss for words, taking the backlash personally. It was one thing to hear someone say that what my father did for a living was weird. It was something else for friends to poke fun at me.

My hunting high quickly evaporated. Frankly, I didn't know how to respond. Not a confrontational person by nature, I felt uncomfortable and unsure of how to stick up for the choice I had made. So I opted for the easy way out. I faked a smile and changed the subject.

But I left the restaurant feeling ashamed. By not asserting my opinion and, instead, going with the flow, in essence I was agreeing with my friends' judgments. I didn't need to respond aggressively, but I could have handled the situation better. I could have pointed to the chicken, beef, and seafood on their plates and asked my fellow diners where they thought their meat came from. I could have explained the basic premise of hunting, educating them about how hunters are actually the biggest conservation group in the world and raise the most money for wildlife preservation. I could have pointed out that specifically in Africa, responsible hunting provides jobs for locals and helps feed their families.

But, hey, I was new at this, trying to figure out if it was even possible to blend two things in my life that I really loved—dancing and hunting—in a way that worked, in a way that didn't paint me as a complete outsider.

Later, I decided it didn't matter what other people thought. I have the power to decide my own destiny. If I let negative remarks from people who don't understand get me down, I am choosing to get in my own way.

André Gide said, "Fear of ridicule begets the worst cowardice."[3] It's human nature to want to be accepted, but that doesn't mean you should let that desire make every decision for you. To go in a new, different direction, I had to trust myself. I had to push against the grain. I had to follow my heart, even if that meant wrestling through the expectations I placed on certain hunts that were left unmet.

4

THE LONGEST DAY

Adopt the pace of nature: her secret is patience.[1]

—RALPH WALDO EMERSON

SASKATCHEWAN, CANADA, 2009

>>

Dusk is falling fast.

Swaddled in the heavy silence of a deer blind,* I can hear the low whistle of wind weaving through the timberline. Thickets of aspen and poplar sweep across the horizon before me. The skinny branches are bare, having long since shed their last few golden and russet leaves. Even through the six-inch opening in the blind, I can see the eerie glow cast on the trees by the setting sun. I hear a bird taking flight, the high chirping of another as it lands nearby. And inside my blind, in this temple of darkness, the quiet burns through me, awakening my spirit to the beauty of nature. Stillness. Peace.

---

* A deer blind is a secluded place where hunters hide to avoid detection, whether a pop-up tent, otherwise known as a ground blind, or a platform (a "stand") secured in a tree.

Nature is my cathedral, where I come face-to-face with creation and Creator. Whether scanning for moose from a willow-blanketed hill in the Yukon or hiking on a parched African plain, I'm ever in God's country. In the quiet of that blind, I inhale the bitter cold Saskatchewan air, then exhale slowly—my mind, my body, and my breath in tune with God.

Okay, okay, okay. Confession time. While every single word of this is true, this ethereal moment did not happen the first time I went on a white-tailed-deer hunt in Saskatchewan. It happened the second season, when I embraced patience and learned that the art of hunting encompasses more than just the harvest. My first trip, on the other hand, almost made me want to give up. But the story of that trip is worth telling, because in hunting—as in life—sometimes the thing you need most isn't the thing you went looking for.

› › ›

In November 2009, I help Dad organize a trip to Saskatchewan, where I will hunt white-tailed deer on the two-thousand-acre property we own there. Mom is coming with us. Here's a fun fact: In 1900, fewer than half a million white-tailed deer remained in the United States. Today, conservation programs have returned the whitetail population to some 32 million.[2]

On the way to Saskatchewan, I ask Dad to tell me about one of his favorite whitetail hunts.

He is all too eager to answer. "Ah, there was the time the biggest buck of my life showed up on the very last day of the season, right in front of me. He came out of the woods and

just stood there at thirty yards, giving me a perfect broadside*
shot." Dad's eyes light up as he continues. "But, Eve, it's not
just about getting the monster buck. It's about how incredible it is to watch deer go about their business in their natural
habitat, unaware we're even there."

Inspired by his story, I'm excited.

Before arriving at the house on our property, I make a pit
stop at Walmart for groceries, a hunting license, and a tag**
for a buck, a male deer. We always hunt selectively, focusing
on mature bucks who are almost or already past breeding age.
These older fellas have spent plenty of years spreading their
seed, so at this point, it's all downhill for them. Their health
will only worsen as they try to survive harsh winters and
predators. Harvesting mature bucks also gives younger males
the opportunity to impress the does and breed their genetics
into the next generation of offspring.

Pushing the bright blue shopping cart up and down the
aisles, I toss in granola bars, boxes of hot chocolate, and pre-
cut veggies. After making my way to the sporting-goods
counter, I stand still, rapt. Surrounding me like an impen-
etrable fortress are displays brimming with hand and foot
warmers, bear sprays, folding shovels, and an assortment of
guns. I gulp. *This is getting real.*

---

* An animal that is broadside, or standing sideways, is the preferred position for shot placement and the shortest distance to vital organs.

** For every hunt, a hunter must purchase a license (required for anyone
carrying a gun or bow) and a tag (a permit that allows the hunter to harvest
a specific species).

I have a bad habit of being hard on myself. I've always been this way. I hate making mistakes. I hate failing. I hate disappointing others. And yet, despite these fears, I also make conscious choices to take risks that have high potentials for failure. While at times anxiety or pressure can be overwhelming, they can also motivate me. They push me to work harder and do my best. When I first started hunting—and even still—I didn't want to let anyone down. Along with Dad, a number of individuals from our family business, including our cameraman, had invested time, energy, and effort into making a hunt possible. I didn't want to disappoint them by saying something dumb, spooking an animal, or, most important, making a bad shot and wounding one.

Around dinnertime, my parents and I arrive at their modestly sized Saskatchewan ranch house, its white siding faded and chipped from years of being exposed to the elements. Nestled on flatland accentuated by the occasional poplar tree, the structure is surrounded by sky and dried golden fields everywhere you look. I've been here many times, plodding through heavy snow on walks with Mom. We'd venture into town to visit my grandmother, where we'd sip hot tea in front of a roaring fireplace. Tomorrow will not provide any of these familiar pleasures. For me, at least.

Before settling in for the night, Dad and I review the trail-camera photos captured near each blind. Let me back up a bit. At this point in the story, as a novice hunter, I don't realize how much work it takes to make a white-tailed-deer hunt happen. Over decades of hunting this land, my dad has figured out where the deer generally are and how they move. Someone, usually my dad, sets up ten to twelve blinds each hunting season accordingly. This happens months before the actual hunt, so the deer can become used to seeing the structures and not be alarmed by them. Then there are the cameras. We want to see which bucks (and how big) are out there. Motion-activated trail cameras are placed on trees near each blind in hopes of recording deer movement. While today these cameras offer great-quality video footage, back when I started hunting, it was just still photos. These cameras are regularly monitored, the memory cards reviewed and new ones inserted, and batteries replaced.

Back to that first night. As Dad and I scroll through the photos, we notice a few mature bucks meandering about, does (female deer), and young bucks, too. The motion sensors also picked up a few coyotes.

Dad points to one of our blinds on the screen. "That one looks like the one with the most deer activity." Most likely it will become our crash pad for the bulk of the following day.

"Check the weather report, Eva."

I click away on the computer keyboard. "Tomorrow's going to get colder. Should be a north wind in the morning and more of a northwest wind toward afternoon. Hopefully that'll get the deer moving."

Many of our blinds are intentionally arranged facing different directions. So, depending on which way the wind is blowing, we'd likely have at least one blind where the wind is coming from the woods toward us, delivering the scent of the wild to us rather than the other way around. This is what it means to "hunt the wind." Since deer depend on their supersonic noses for survival and can catch the scent of a human a quarter of a mile away, it's crucial to be on the right side of the wind at all times.

Two hours later I lie in bed, wrapped in a wool blanket. The window to my right ushers in the soft glow of moonlight. Eyes closed, I picture Mom's face, her beaming smile. I'm torn, knowing that in the morning I'll leave her and go off with Dad for the day. I love the traditional role Mom plays in our family. It's a big part of who she is. The part of me that appreciates her way of life and her choices connects us, brings us closer. My mind toys with guilt over the pull I feel toward the unconventional, the desire to explore Dad's very un-girlish world.

Why can't I have both? Why does it have to be one or the other?

> > >

Having slept for, at best, a handful of hours, Dad and I leave the house the next morning when it's still dark. The minute I step outside, the sharp wind blasts my face. Hunting in this part of the world is not for the faint of heart. The cold bludgeons its way through my fleece and wool layers, the chill seeping into my bones. During this time, the temperature can reach as low as thirty degrees below zero, Fahrenheit, with the wind chill making it feel like fifty below.

We drive for about ten minutes. Though I'm still adjusting to the early wake-up call, I'm bursting with eager chatter. When Dad switches off the engine, he looks me up and down. "If I were you, I'd take off a few layers."

Thinking the frigid temperature is making him crazy, I shake my head. "No way. I'm fine."

Of course, I don't realize that I might get sweaty from the thirty-minute walk into the woods to reach our blind and that sweat will spark a day-long freeze of my body. I would learn by the end of the day that I could either be uncomfortably cold for a half hour during the morning hike or cold and shivering for the next twelve hours.

I hop out of the truck, the cold piercing through my clothing to my skin. I'm grateful I'm wearing two pairs of long underwear, fleece sweatpants, hunting pants, and more layers of fleece and wool on top.

"Okay, no more talking," Dad says. "Deer can be anywhere."

I look around. The empty field is enveloped by darkness, lit only by the moon beaming down on us. While we can't see them, deer, with their superior night vision, can see us. Silence is now golden and key to staying undetected. Even in the blind, the smallest whisper or the unwrapping of a granola bar can spark the attention of an otherwise unsuspecting doe or buck nearby.

After quietly unloading our gear, headlamps strapped to our foreheads, we begin the thirty-minute speed walk to the blind, our boots crunching on the frost-covered ground and the occasional dry branch. I hold my rolled-up Heater Body Suit (HBS) firmly with one gloved hand. This camouflage-patterned and insulated sleeping bag is a godsend in the shivering-in-your-bones, icicles-on-your-eyelashes, lips-turning-into-ice-blocks kind of cold.

The muzzleloader is slung over my shoulder, and in the crook of my arm I'm carrying a beach chair, where I'll stay planted for the duration of the day. My backpack is strapped on tightly, filled with an ungodly amount of extra fleece and wool layers, binoculars, and some unwrapped snacks. A quarter of a mile in, I start to sweat. This thin layer of wetness stays damp for the next twelve hours. To this day, I've never worn extra layers on the hike again.

We're hunting in November during the rut, or mating season. During this time of the year, bucks can be pretty unpredictable when trying to pair up with does. Within legal hunting hours (in Saskatchewan it's thirty minutes before sunup until thirty minutes after sundown), they tend to move the most during the later afternoon into the evening but can show up at any time of the day. It's best to stay put in a blind from before dawn until after dusk and wait.

Let's talk rut. Before female deer enter their estrus cycle, pre-rut, bucks mostly stick together in bachelor posses. Once the rut hits, the females start being fertile, and the bucks split up and start chasing does down. They shadow the ladies, testing the waters for receptivity. As soon as a buck finds a willing doe to breed with, the two couple up. Then the buck is off again, looking for another doe in heat. It's nonstop action for the bucks. They're so busy, they barely stop long enough to eat.

About an hour and a half before sunup, we crawl into the five-foot-diameter circular pop-up blind lightly covered by brushwood; the skinny twigs and branches help the weatherproof, camouflage-patterned tent blend into the natural environment. I put down my stuff as Dad sets up in silence. He positions our chairs on opposite sides of the blind, both facing the two-foot-wide opening across the front of the tent so we can watch from different angles and get a broader view of our surrounding area. Tying up black towels with twine, he then swiftly patches up every inch of space in the blind where light could trickle in. Other important items, such as binoculars and batteries, are unpacked to be placed in our laps or at the feet of the beach chairs for easy access. I stay out of his way, but I watch every move Dad makes. The next day, I plan to lend a hand.

Finally, we climb into our six-pound Michelin Man–like sleeping bags. Arms contained inside, we zip them up slowly from the inside with the least noise possible. With the last *zzzzz* of the metal zippers, it's time to sit down and shut up. My muzzleloader, already loaded and with the safety on, rests on the Primos Trigger Sticks in front of my chair. With just the tip of the barrel sticking out of the blind's opening and the butt of the gun parked comfortably on my lap, I'm ready for action.

Hunting whitetail in Saskatchewan bears no resemblance to hunting warthogs in South Africa. Unlike a spot-and-stalk hunt, where I canvass mountains, fields, or valleys for an animal and then strategically approach it, hunting white-tailed deer involves sitting quietly in a small tent, ground blind, or tree stand for about twelve hours straight, hoping the animal I'm looking for wanders into my view. The only motion on my part is the thirty-minute hike to the blind.

Dad waves a hand to catch my attention and whispers,

"Once the sun comes up, we should start to see some movement." Finally, silence. No more talking. No zipping. No rustling with equipment or gear. Definitely no light.

I nod, stifling a yawn. I'm exhausted. Feels silly to be so tired when the day hasn't even begun. The wind blows into the blind, biting into the top part of my face. Still half asleep and with about an hour of downtime before the sun will creep its way over the horizon, I slouch back into the chair, chin tucked deep into the HBS. Knowing a catnap will do wonders before the party starts, I close my eyes.

❯ ❯ ❯

Day breaks gently. As the sky unfolds its arms in a vibrant display of oranges, reds, and pinks, the scene outside the blind opening begins to lighten. Thorny thickets, their branches tangled with one another, accompany the tall, skinny poplar and aspen trees that dot the horizon. Underneath, a blanket of frozen earth is tipped with frost. Silence is swept away by the chorus of songbirds. Squirrels and chipmunks dart over and under dead logs, the bark stripped bare in spots. But while the outside world begins to resurrect with light and color, we sit silently in the dark. And we wait for a mature buck to come into view.

Our senses are heightened to detect the slightest sound. Whenever a twig snaps, branches crackle, or a pile of parched leaves crunches under the weight of something, I perk up. It might signal the entrance of the biggest buck in all of Saskatchewan. But not today. The source of branches rattling in the wind comes from black-billed magpies flapping their wings in flight from one tree to the next. And the twigs snapping? Nothing more than a skittish squirrel. Small animals have a way of puncturing hope.

Two hours pass.

Sitting. Watching. Waiting. No buck.

Four hours.

Sitting. Watching. Waiting. Still no buck.

Tick. Tock. Tick. Tock. Tick. Tock.

I reach into my jacket pocket for an unwrapped, fuzz-covered granola bar. I break a piece off and, reaching up through the neck opening of the HBS, pop it into my mouth. I chew quietly, the peanut butter and chocolate chips melting in my mouth. And I continue to sit. Watch. And wait.

No buck. No doe. Zilch. Zero. Nada.

This sucks! Where are the deer? What time is it? How much longer do we have to stay here? It's hard to stay positive. I search high and low for the silver lining somewhere within this hair-pulling stretch of monotony but can't find it. I'm cold. I'm tired. And I'm doing absolutely nothing. The only thing that keeps me somewhat sane is calculating how many snacks I can eat and when, based on how many are in my pocket and how much time we have left. Counting down the minutes to my next edible treat turns out to be the biggest highlight of the day.

The way Dad described whitetail hunting seemed exciting. I had looked forward to seeing deer bounding along with their graceful gaits and slender necks or standing motionless, on high alert, flicking their white tails. My expectations are betrayed by a very uneventful day.

At around one thirty, with about four-plus hours left to hunt, I start counting down the minutes. Dumb mistake. This doesn't help the situation at all. It just makes time seem to drag even more slowly. When it's time to call it a day, I'm sorely disappointed. What a letdown!

The minute I climb into Dad's truck and close the passenger door, I unleash twelve hours of pent-up disdain for whitetail hunting. "This was probably the most boring day of my life! Why didn't you warn me nothing would happen? I feel like I just wasted twelve hours of my life!"

Dad smiles knowingly as I continue to vent my frustration. "I don't think I can do this again. Twelve hours without moving? Twelve hours without seeing anything?! Twelve hours of being cold and miserable for absolutely no reason?!"

"Eve, hunting whitetail is a game of patience. You're going to be cold. You're going to be hungry. You're going to be tired. And you might not see anything for a week straight or even an entire hunting season sometimes. A buck might not show up until the last hour of the last day, but when he does, you have to be ready."

I nod, trying hard not to roll my eyes. With a dramatic sigh, I peel off my outer fleece layers as the truck blasts a rush of heat that begins to thaw my extremities.

Dad continues his spiel of encouragement. "You have to look at the positive things, Eve. Listen to the forest come alive. Watch the birds play. Breathe in the fresh air." My father tries to paint a different picture of hunting, reminding me that it's not just about the harvest. It's about the adventure of being in the center of nature and wildlife and being grateful to be alive and awake in God's cathedral. It's about finding the beauty, however subtle, in the outdoors—watching a leaf give up its bright green color to the tune of autumn gold, or feeling the gentle breath of wind that blows through your hair unseen, or watching shadows dance on trees when the sun melts into night.

I nod, trying, really trying, to embrace his perspective, but at my core, unease grows. Especially when we walk into the house, which is draped in the aroma of my mom's famous herb-roasted chicken and spicy deer chili. Cozy and stunning in her wool sweater after a day of relaxation and warmth, Mom wraps her arms around me in a bear hug. "How did it go?" she asks as I inhale the sweet scent of her Chanel N°5 perfume. It reminds me I need a shower.

Washing up before dinner, with Dad gone, I break down. "It was long. It was cold. We didn't see anything. It wasn't fun. I don't know how Dad does it day after day. I wish I'd stayed home with you and Grandma." Now I'm fighting tears.

"Oh. Well, just give it a chance. It will get better," she assures me. "Your dad always says that hunting is about patience." She pauses for a second and continues. "Well, me and Grandma sure missed you today. We went shopping at that new antiques store in town and found the sweetest little decorations for Grandma's house for Christmas. If you get your deer soon, you can come help us put them up this week!"

But her attempts at encouragement don't encourage. In fact, the disparity between her day and mine alarms me. A newbie whitetail hunter, I have no context for sitting in a dark blind for twelve hours. For me, at this point, I don't think it's worth it. *What am I doing here?* I wonder, second-guessing my decision to hunt. *I'm missing out on spending time with Mom and Grandma.* On one hand, I was learning the art of hunting and enjoying quality, one-on-one time with Dad; on the other hand, it was slow—I mean, *s-l-o-w*—and boring. I wondered if I made the right decision. While the reality of my experience was nothing more than one bad day of hunting, I interpreted it as a red flag. Maybe I was wrong. Maybe hunting wasn't in my DNA after all.

In the spirit of transparency, I'll admit that I still get this feeling whenever I get frustrated on a hunting trip. There are times when I'm tired, hungry, and extra uncomfortable from the elements. There are times when I miss my husband and the comforts of home. There are times when everything that can possibly go wrong on a hunt does. In those moments, no matter how much I try to fight the negativity that seeps into my mind, I question my love for hunting. Shouldn't it be stronger than how bad I'm feeling? I know I'm lucky to be outdoors. I know I'm blessed to be able to hunt. But it's not easy to always stay optimistic and remain focused on the bigger picture of being able to do what I love. When I was growing up, my parents urged me to do something with my life that I loved 80 percent of the time. "No matter what you choose," they said, "it's not going to be perfect. There will be days you don't like it or it's hard or boring. But if you're excited about it eighty percent of the time, you can handle the twenty percent that's not so great."

The next morning is more of the same. No action. Huddled in my HBS in another ground blind, I groan.

Oh, my gosh. This cannot be happening again!

Suddenly, at around 11:00 a.m., I hear what sounds like a good-size branch breaking. Dad motions with his hand to get closer to the window while mouthing, "I can hear something!" My heart starts thundering in my chest.

This could be it. This could be it.

Pointing his finger in the direction of the noise, Dad whispers with controlled excitement, "I see it. I see it. Unzip your suit. Get your gun ready. Get in position. It's coming!"

As I ditch my gloves and hand warmers and slowly start unzipping the HBS to waist level, I lean closer to the opening. With my bare eyes, I scan the woods, trying to spot movement or even part of an approaching deer. Nothing yet. Repositioning the gun off my lap and against my shoulder, I look through the scope. My heart pounds. I still don't see anything, but I want to be ready. The anticipation of seeing a colossal buck mosey through an opening in the bare trees drives my adrenaline through the roof.

Then, sixty yards away, I see something through the brush.

It's a doe. Oblivious, she ambles her way toward us, her round body carried by slender limbs. The fact that I have a tag for a buck, instead, tempers some of my excitement. I relax, placing the gun back on my lap. As my heart rate starts to descend, I can't help but watch her. I'm struck speechless, being so close to this elegant creature. I'm able to make out the markings on her fur, the twitching of her pointy ears, her quivering nostrils. Dad, a smile stretched over his face, whispers, "Isn't this cool?" And in that moment, the questions and the fears that had plagued me about hunting vanish. I catch, at the very least, a glimpse of why Dad does what he does.

Seeing that doe forces me to be present. To stop and stare. To marvel at creation. Nursing some reservations, I still am not entirely sold on whitetail hunting. But my mind-set shifts into a better place. Instead of tuning in to how boring this hunt is, I start to focus on what is in front of me—in that moment, a beautiful doe. Even if she's not the deer I've been waiting for, it's still pretty cool.

I watch her for a good thirty minutes. Nose to the ground, she nibbles on a frozen shrub for a while, then raises her head. Her ears twitch, attuned to a suspicious sound. Suddenly, eyes wide as if she's seen a ghost, the doe freezes. Then, moving her head gracefully from side to side, she starts stomping the earth with one foot.

"Just wait," Dad whispers. "She sees or hears something. This is good! There could be a buck coming in! Get ready!"

I take off the gloves I had just put back on and place the butt of the gun back against my shoulder, eye to the scope. Within the next few seconds, I see movement. Another brown mass, concealed slightly by a thicket similar in color. As I hop back onto the emotional roller coaster, my heart resumes its wild beating. Through the lens I can see a muscled thigh, then a brown torso slowly moving toward the doe. I swallow hard, gun ready, as a long neck comes into view.

"Get ready, Eve. Breathe. Just breathe. I'll tell you if it's a shooter," Dad whispers.

My breathing feels amplified. I try to quiet the ragged sound.

Then the anticipation shatters into nothingness. It's another doe.

The two females stand within ten feet of each other, heads down, looking for wisps of dry grass to chew. It's a beautiful sight. Two lovely ladies grazing, attentive to their surroundings but unhurried, unaware of who might be watching. I'm somewhat disappointed that the second sighting isn't a buck, but I'm not about to ruin the moment with unnecessary frustration. As I stare out of the blind, I shift in my seat. The gun accidentally slips ever so slightly off my lap and clinks the aluminum part of my chair. Game over. The pair of deer resumes high alert. They start stomping their hooves on the ground. Dad shakes his head. By the time I can reposition the muzzleloader, the does bound out of sight. I feel foolish knowing I spooked them, but it was a lesson in how quiet I have to be.

The next six days are a blur of more of the same. I see a few does here and there and a buck or two with tiny antlers, too young to shoot. In the last few hours of day eight, the day closes fast without any opportunities. Down to the wire, knowing how much time others had invested setting up the blinds and trail cams and the long hours I'd put in myself, I can't help but be disappointed.

And then, as dusk approaches, it's time to go home.

My backpack is nestled tightly against my body, gun and

beach chairs slung over my shoulders. Just like the last seven nights. Except this time, I'm not coming back in the morning. I leave the woods without tagging the antlers of a buck, without heaping his heavy body onto the truck to be skinned and dressed in the skinning shed on the farm. No deer meat for the winter. My first whitetail experience in Saskatchewan is a bust. My heart is heavy. I can't help but revisit my earlier doubts. *Maybe I'm not cut out for this.*

Riding back to the farmhouse, Dad tries his best to encourage me. "Eve, this is part of hunting. We don't do it just to shoot. Many of the best hunters in the world leave without animals."

"Uh-huh," I mutter, turning my face to look out the window. We drive through the bumpy field, the sky almost faded of color. "Dad, I'm just not sure I want to do this again."

"You have to remember that deer do what they want, when they want, and how they want. It doesn't matter if you're hunting on the best property or you have fifty years' experience, you can't control these animals. Just put in the time, Eve. We'll try against next fall."

I face him and force a feeble smile. Truth is, I'm not so sure. Deer hunting seems too slow for my taste. I function at a fast pace. When I want to do something, I do it. When there's a problem, I fix it. When I set a goal, I do everything in my power to reach it. I don't usually sit around waiting for things to happen. It's a tough personality to have as a hunter.

Even though the advice from Dad somewhat opens my eyes to appreciate little things, I still can't find the positive in spending so much time doing something without anything to show for it. I determine not to go on another whitetail hunt ever again.

Preparing for my flight home the next morning, doubt simmers. I sit on the edge of the bed, trying to come to grips with the experience. Did I expect to shoot a monster on my first run? Did I really think every single second of every single hunt would be fun and amazing and exciting? Do I decide hunting isn't my thing and walk away? Or do I suck it up and keep at it?

Though I still cling to a smidgen of bitterness about the hunt, I can't imagine my future without hunting. I can't imagine not getting to spend a week with my parents in Saskatchewan and shooting my gun and checking trail cameras. I can't imagine not giving myself another chance to wait for the elusive buck that outsmarted us.

In life, as in deer hunting, there is always an opportunity to give up. There's always a chance to choose the path of least resistance and come up with an excuse to call it quits. These are the moments that define us and mold our lives. Our future is dependent on our present choices. That day in Saskatchewan, a big part of me wanted to quit hunting and return to my familiar comforts. But I knew if I walked away, I would have failed myself. And I would never have known what was possible. In hindsight, I realize that I was completely missing the fact that hunting is about the experience and not necessarily the end result. I'm thankful I chose to stay in the game.

I left the farmhouse knowing I'd be back next year. It's

ironic. Today, whitetail hunting in Saskatchewan is one of my favorite things to do.

You never know what God has in store for you when you hang in there. We all have doubts. We all have moments of frustration. We all question what we're doing sometimes. But it's often in these moments, when we least expect it, that something happens. Change comes. Maybe our situation changes. Or maybe we do.

› › ›

Two months later, I ride the escalator in the Sands Expo Center in Las Vegas, Nevada. It's the opening of trade-show season, 2010. Tens of thousands of outdoor enthusiasts gather throughout the almost 2.5-million-square-foot space. My first hunt in Africa had recently aired on our TV show. I watched the episode in the editing suite. I don't think most people enjoy watching themselves on camera. I know I didn't. But though I looked awkward and uncomfortable on camera, I was proud of myself for following through with the hunt.

I was now confident in my choice to lock arms with the hunting community. Still, a part of me worried what professionals in the industry would think, particularly the few women hunters I did know. Would they assume I was trying to steal Dad's thunder? Or, worse, steal theirs? Would they peg me as an opportunist riding her father's coattails just to be on TV?

On the expo floor, I walk through the crowds, waving

and saying hello in passing to those I know, smiling past strangers. Intermingled in the crowd are hunters who have been in the industry for ten or more years, along with a ton of outdoor TV hosts. I feel small, out of place. My palms start to sweat. Imagine my surprise when I run into Tiffany Lakosky, a fellow female hunter who has a successful show on Outdoor Channel. Flashing a beautiful smile, she throws her arms wide open and hugs me. "I saw your episode, Eva. It was great! It's so awesome that you're hunting with your dad!" I blush. What an honor.

Tiffany is respected by many, myself included. I'm grateful for the time she spends with me, sharing her excitement about my decision to start hunting. That day other pros in the industry do the same. They wish me well and offer to answer any questions I may have. Getting affirmed is humbling. It means a lot. It tells me that new hunters are welcomed and embraced, not frowned upon or shunned. I begin to feel at home in this new world.

Being at the trade show also got me thinking. Made me reflect on what I was doing day in and day out and what I wanted my future to look like. While I didn't come up with answers for everything, I knew it was time to consider some options. I loved nannying, but it wasn't a career path I wanted to venture down for the next thirty years. I loved dancing, but it wasn't going to pay the bills or allow me the flexibility to travel and hunt. I wanted to do something that was bigger than me, that meant something, that I enjoyed doing.

A week later, I had a sit-down with Dad and Dan Goodenow, the VP of sales in Dad's company who sold, planned, and organized the hunts. With a heart as big as they come, Dan was a great hunter and had sharp business acumen.

I sat in front of these two men in Dad's home office. I rubbed my bare feet on the soft surface of a gold-flecked grizzly-bear rug and said, "I go to these trade shows year after year, and I love them more and more each time. But I have no idea what my role is here. I want to feel like I have a purpose here, that I'm doing something useful."

I was hired as an event manager and joined the family business, Dad's outfitting company, which included about thirty men and women, some part-time, some full. To avoid things getting weird with Dad as my boss, we all agreed I would work directly for Dan. Having known him for years and what a stand-up guy he was, I was excited to learn from him. I coordinated our annual charity golf event, organized our trade-show booths, oversaw the rebranding and redesign of our website, created Shockey-branded merchandise like hats and shirts, dabbled in branding, and did some admin work—pretty much whatever was needed.

Though I didn't realize it at the time, accepting the job offer was one of the most life-changing decisions I'd make. I can see now what I couldn't then. I was walking through an open door, leaving one world behind and inviting another to reveal itself.

5

INTO THE WOODS

Experience is what you get when you didn't get
what you wanted.[1]

—RANDY PAUSCH

NORTHERN VANCOUVER ISLAND, 2010

The salty Pacific air lures me in, intoxicating. It's May, and I've just arrived at bear camp. A row of red-roofed cabins lines a stretch of pebbled beach where, as a little girl, I'd spent hours hunting for smooth, colored stones. But this time, I'd hike the mountains on my first spot and stalk for a black bear.

I arrive armed with a muzzleloader and a new bow. I've been a member at the local archery club back home for about a year. With lanes filled with men and women, young and old, drawing their bows, I'd felt right at home—except for the fact that I was the only one holding a camo-colored one, a dead giveaway that I was a hunter. For some reason, that slight detail elicited many raised eyebrows and weird looks from fellow shooters. Seemed archery practice was acceptable for city dwellers, as long as it wasn't for the purpose of hunting.

I tried to shoot at least once a week. Often, I'd have to force myself to get to the range. Being indoors was stifling. I preferred instead to practice outdoors, breathing fresh air and feeling the sun on my face. Also, shooting with real-life hunting elements, such as wind and natural light, made more sense to me. Further, the archery club provided limited targets, only at the ten- and twenty-yard marks, while shooting outdoors gave me the option to practice both close and far shots. So every two weeks or so, I'd pack up my bow and head out to my childhood home, where I'd shoot using Block Targets, a brand of cube-shaped, high density, foam-filled archery targets, as far away as fifty yards. I wasn't necessarily comfortable shooting an animal that far away, but practicing and gaining confidence at fifty yards makes shooting twenty yards in a high-pressure hunting situation much easier.

Good archery skill requires building muscle memory. When you hunt with a firearm, assuming your gun is sighted-in correctly and you can squeeze the trigger slowly and without any jerky movement, you can be pretty accurate. This is true if you practice two hours a day or only for two minutes. A bow is much different. Most archers will agree that practice is directly related to consistent accuracy. Every minute I shoot my bow brings me a little bit closer to where I want to be.

I'll let you in on a secret: I don't always love practicing. There are a hundred other things that I can think of doing with my time: catching up on e-mails, doing laundry, going to the gym, cooking dinner, seeing friends, returning phone calls. But I know that I'm accountable for my goals. I want to shoot my bow accurately at twenty, thirty, and forty yards. Not just sometimes. I want to make a good shot every single time. And these things won't happen if I don't practice.

Side note. Although I brought my bow on this trip intending to hunt with it, I never broke the twenty-five-yard distance with any bear. I couldn't even think of shooting one any farther away than that. The muzzleloader was my accompaniment, ready for action when a likely harvest was out of range for my bow.

The morning after we arrive at bear camp, Dad is shifting gears on the two-hour drive toward our hunting area. Matt, our cameraman on this trip, is accompanying us today. We always have one with us on every hunt. The rugged-terrain tires spin over some jagged rocks and hit the mini cross ditch stretched along the width of the road. I bounce hard in the passenger seat, my head crashing into the roof of the truck.

I need to get used to riding on these roads. For over forty years, logging trucks have barreled down these same narrow tracks, hauling away massive ancient Douglas fir and red and yellow cedar and leaving behind open sky and scarred hillsides strewn with slash, which is a mixture of stumps and logging debris. Some of the slash are burned to clear forest. But without intending to, the loggers make a paradise for bears. The maze of rotting logs, piles of dead tree limbs, and blackened stumps form hideaways where black bears love to explore and take naps.

Shifting in my seat, I kick my backpack. It's filled with moleskin, Band-Aids, and a tag for a black bear. Ascending toward the honey hole of bear hunting via logging roads,

I'm on the lookout for a male, or boar. This is not an easy thing to determine in the field unless a bear is in a position that exposes its underside, and that rarely happens. While a boar is usually bigger than a female, or sow, they generally look the same, so I have to pay attention to other clues. For instance, if you see a black bear with small cubs nearby, it's a sow. Boars are never around cubs except when they want to eat them. Some scientists believe that during mating season (rut), a boar will kill the cubs near a sow he's interested in to bring her into heat sooner. There are more clues. Boars are usually beefier than females and walk with a swagger, clomping along on all fours with dominance and aggression. They have big drooping noses (what we call Roman noses). Their ears, often shredded from fights with other boars, appear small in relation to their wide heads. Females are more petite, but their ears are bigger compared to their narrow faces. They are also more shy and cautious. But in the wild, as in life, you'll find exceptions to every rule. Since that first time hunting bears, I've seen many large "boars" that were actually sows upon closer inspection through the spotting scope, a compact telescope that offers more magnification power than binoculars.

We're hunting during the rut, the best time to hunt animals. Male bears are especially combative during this time. They have one month to do all their breeding. Pumped up with testosterone and aggression, they're on the prowl for females. They will not put up with competitors. Grappling with pulverizing force, slashing with razor-sharp claws, male bears will fight to the death any intruding boars who try to mate with their females. In other words, they are far from the cute and cuddly creatures portrayed in certain toilet-paper commercials.

"Watch out for busted trees," Dad points out, navigating the old gravel logging road with precision. "The boars break saplings to mark their territory."

"Uh-huh." I make a mental note of this fact, but I'm focused, eyes wide, on the blind corner he's careering around. It's as if Dad doesn't notice that the truck is hugging the mountain on one side and mere inches from a two-hundred-foot drop on the other.

Pointing to the vegetation sprouting on the sides of the road, Dad says, "Bears like to eat clover and salmonberries. They'll dig for insects that burrow in the stumps, too." My crash course in Bear Hunting 101 continues. "Never get in the way of a sow and her cubs. A sow can get really aggressive when she thinks her cubs are in danger.

"Oh, and be sure you make a good shot the first time. A wounded bear will make for a disastrous situation if you have to go into thick bush looking for it."

We get out of the truck at a lookout point. The air is moistened by a light drizzle, the temperature comfortable in the upper forties. Peering intently through my binoculars, I try to find a black blob of bear among the black blobs of tree stumps and castaway logs. There are no bears in my line of sight. I feast, instead, on the breathtaking scene around me. A vast canopy of old-growth fir and hemlock trees shelters the valleys below, neighbored by the occasional logging slash. Crooked ravines spiral through low ground. Vibrant Indian paintbrush flowers and alder trees line the sides of the logging roads that snake up, around, and down the mountain. As I marvel at nature's finest handiwork, a bald eagle swoops low. Less than fifty feet in front of me, its talons are outstretched, ready to snatch a small critter for a mid-morning snack. Circle of life.

Then my awe-fest gets cut short.

"Look down there." Dad points down into the valley, binoculars in hand. "I see two. One big, one smaller. I can't tell if it's a boar with a sow or a sow with a cub."

Whipping out a spotting scope, he digs its tripod legs into the dirt and gets a closer look. "It sure looks like a big boar with a sow," Dad says with excitement.

I know what's next. I grab the gun and the shooting sticks out of the truck and set out on foot with him back down the mountain. We pace a light jog on the winding and uneven road, feet crashing down over fine bits of slash and small limbs. Down and around we hustle, then slow to stalk toward the spot we last saw the bears.

Bears have poor long-distance eyesight. They make up for this with an uncanny sense of smell. In fact, with the sharpest sense of any walking mammal in North America, they can smell 2,100 times better than a human can. Getting close to these bears is one thing. Making sure we're on the right side of the wind is another. Enter wind-indicator powder. Don't think of a special product you can only buy at a hunting store. Think inexpensive, unscented, talcum powder on a shelf at your corner pharmacy. As we walk, Dad squeezes the powder into the air. By following where the white dust goes, we can determine which way the wind is blowing. The wind might have been against us that day—I can't remember. But we never saw those bears again. My best guess is that they smelled us and hightailed it out of there.

The rest of the day is pretty much a bust. We see two, maybe three, bears, but none is close enough or stays still long enough, not even for the muzzleloader. That night we eat dinner just before midnight. Because the days are long and the mountains a two-hour drive away from camp, dinner is usually served no earlier than 11:00 p.m. Fellow hunters/clients, guides from Dad's outfit, my parents, and I gather around a long, rectangular table in the mess hall. A cacophony of male voices booms over clanking silverware. Between chewing mouthfuls of baked potatoes oozing with melting butter and grilled salmon caught earlier in the day, the men share the day's tales.

"I put a stalk on the biggest bear I've ever seen! We got up to two hundred yards, and right when we came around the corner on the logging path, he was facing us dead-on and had us pegged. He spun around so fast and crashed into the thick bush before I even had a chance to get my gun ready," one hunter narrated.

And another: "I was at full draw* on a monster boar at thirty-five yards. My whole body was shaking. I could barely breathe or think. But he just wouldn't give me a shot. The bear was moving through the slash, and there was a bush in

* Full draw is when a bow is pulled back to its maximum extension and ready to shoot.

front of him, and I just didn't have a clear window to shoot. I don't know how long I stayed at full draw, but eventually I had to let down my bow because I was shaking so bad. He never gave me a shot after that. I was gutted!"

Surrounded by men, most in their mid-forties or older, I feel awkward. As if I don't belong or even deserve to sit next to them as they swap dramatic stories. No one says anything in particular to highlight the pink elephant in the room, but no one has to. It's obvious. The masculine energy in the dining hall is palpable. Many of these hunters are on their annual "boys" trips, away from wives and children. The time together offers shared camaraderie, a space for untamed tongues. No need to worry about offending the fairer sex. My presence in this dynamic is a bit jarring.

Maybe if I tuck my long blond ponytail inside the collar of my hunting jacket or lose the mascara tomorrow, I'll fit in. I'm reminded of the time my dance friends tossed around passive-aggressive comments about my hunting. Aware that it's my own insecurity working against me, I fight my feelings. I want to do what I love without being perceived as weird or misunderstood. If others view me as an outsider, who cares? Apparently, I do.

Comments from my peers during my childhood ring in my ears. "Hunting is a man's sport." "Girls who hunt are butch." "Girls aren't tough enough to handle the wilderness." These statements reflect ignorance and have no merit, but they're hard to tune out. Yet what choice do I have? If I surrender to my insecurity and dial in to the whispers or loud-mouthed opinions that female hunters do not belong in the field, I know what will happen. I'll call it quits, hang up my bow and gun, and do something else.

As I chew on a warm, buttered roll, I remind myself how much I love to hunt. And in that moment, as the mental gymnastics begin to subside, I realize that that's all that matters. I'm doing what I love. I'm doing what I'm finally starting to believe I'm meant to do. And if I look out of place at this dinner table with bear-hunting colleagues, so what?

Just as I silence my internal monologue, another hunter is finishing a story. ". . . these cubs looked like little black footballs with four tiny legs apiece. There must have been a sow nearby."

I hope the next day I get to share a story of my own.

> > >

My second day of bear hunting gets more exciting. As Dad and I drive up a logging road early in the morning, I notice a few broken branches by the side of the road. I abandon the truck to get a closer look. Moving through the alder and noting the jagged stubs of broken tree limbs, I'm seeing what appears to be the handiwork of an aggressive male bear. And, judging by how high the splintered branches are, a pretty big one. Looks like six or seven feet standing up on its hind legs.

Hoping we're hot on the bear's trail, we hustle on foot up the side of the mountain. Taking on the role of official wind-checker, I squeeze the bottle of talcum powder into the air. Puffs of white dust swirl toward us. I then spot a black blob in the distance. It moves closer, swelling in size to a massive creature covered in coarse fur. The bear schleps along the road ahead of us, guarding his territory from infiltrators. He stops, standing broadside at eighty yards. Opportunity is ripe.

Dad plants the Trigger Sticks into the ground. "There you go, Eve," he whispers. "Get your gun on the sticks."

I place the muzzleloader in the yoke. The gun doesn't rest naturally against my shoulder. It feels awkward.

"I'm going to try to make him stop again so he gives you a shot," Dad says, preparing to mimic a boar by vocalizing low huffing sounds.

Hunching over uncomfortably to get my eye on the scope, I shake my head. "Wait a second. The sticks are way too low."

Dad pulls on the lever, elevating the height. This time, they're too high. More adjustments. Finally, with the Trigger Sticks just right, I reposition the gun and cock back the hammer. The gun is ready to shoot. With a mixture of excitement and nerves, my heart races. Adrenaline pumps through my body, making it tough to steady my hands. Suddenly, a gust of wind rolls through the air. And it's changed direction, delivering our scent straight to the bear. The animal lifts his big furry head and turns toward us. *Can he see us?* Armed with suspicious curiosity, the bear stands up on his hind legs. His incredible stature gives me pause, resetting the adrenaline rush into overdrive.

"Are you solid?" Dad asks.

"Not even close."

With those words, I watch as the bear gets down on all

fours, and, in a flash, his big body barrels down the hill in a hasty retreat.

Carefully returning the hammer to the safe position, I sigh. Hopes dashed. An experienced hunter would have been ready for the shot. But I needed extra time to get my gun on the sticks and pull the trigger calmly. This is a lesson for me. I have to take responsibility. And I have to be ready. I can't rely on Dad to set everything up for me.

I wonder if he shares my disappointment. To my surprise, Dad puts his arm around me and says, "That's exactly what you needed to do, Eve. Don't take the shot unless you're absolutely ready. You made the right choice. And don't worry, you'll have more chances."

I sling the gun back over my shoulder, heading down the mountain toward the truck.

We see more bears that day, about ten or fifteen, a typical amount for an average spring day. One, up on his hind legs, clawed at the side of a tree. A few mama bears moseyed along, their cubs scampering nearby. Some bears munched on clover or salmonberries. Younger ones clambered up trees with remarkable speed. None of these bears was close enough to shoot, let alone broadside. We arrive at camp late at night. No big tale to tell.

On day four or five, around 6:00 p.m., prime time for bear sightings, Dad and I drive around a bend in the road. A slash appears up the slope on our right. In the last few days, a handful of times I thought I saw a black blob in the thick of the fallen trees and logs. "Bear! Bear!" I'd yell, pointing out the window. Dad would slam on the brakes and look into the slash. All my sightings proved to be tree stumps, not bears. Quite the letdown. I vowed to keep my mouth shut until I was absolutely certain I saw a bear.

But this time, I break my promise. "Bear!" I blurt out.

Based on my record of stump-spotting, Dad is skeptical. "Are you positive, Eva?"

Sure enough, a bear is moving through the slash. We get out of the truck. Muzzleloader on my shoulder and Trigger Sticks in hand, I crouch low behind Dad as we stalk closer. The bear rustles on a hillside three hundred yards away. As we tiptoe closer, I notice its thick upper body. It also has a wide head and little ears. The bear stands up straight and with one massive paw grabs the trunk of a sapling. In a move that demonstrates sheer strength, power, and aggression, the bear snaps it in half. According to the rule book for determining bear gender, it sure seems like a boar.

Stalking along the side of the bushes, we move in closer. Two hundred yards away. As I hurry to close the distance, I happen to look down just before my foot is about to strike the ground. There before me, just inches away from my hiking boot, lies a Coke bottle–size bear dropping. Fresh, green, and, I assume, still warm. Pardon the detail, but big bear scat usually indicates a big male bear.

Confirming my suspicion, Dad says, "Definitely a boar. Get ready."

Trigger Sticks erected, I steady the gun. Through the scope I see the bear tramping over the forest floor, looking for his next conquest. Then, suddenly, he disappears into the maze of stumps and fallen branches. I look around, my eyes scanning all the nearby brush piles. *Where did he go?* Five minutes pass. That's a long time. Long enough for doubt to creep in. *Why is this taking so long? What if I can't get a good shot? What if he turns his back on me and goes in the other direction? What if this is my last chance?* The longer I have to think, the more I start to psych myself out. Suddenly, a shadow: the bear's rounded torso. But I can't see his vitals, where I need to aim. I need a better shot. I grab the gun and move twenty yards to adjust my vantage point. Dad follows, bringing the sticks.

Now I can see more angles of the bear. Settling the muzzleloader into place, I take a deep breath. Then another. My body relaxes, heaving slowly with every breath even though my heart is racing like a locomotive. The bear takes a step and turns sideways. He still doesn't know we're there. Peering through the scope, I groan. Trigger Sticks are too high.

"Can you see him?" Dad whispers.

"Yes, but I gotta move the sticks."

Before Dad has a chance to step in, I solve my own problem by dropping the poles about an inch.

"Are you good?" Dad asks, his naked eye dead center on the bear.

"Yeah, all good."

But I don't have a shot until the bear turns broadside. When he does, Dad whispers, "There you go."

I nod, cocking back the hammer and positioning the crosshairs behind the bear's shoulder. I exhale and squeeze the trigger. The muzzleloader belches smoke. I can't see anything in front of me for a good two seconds. By the time the air is clear, the bear is out of sight.

"How'd the shot feel?" Dad asks, taking a few steps away from me to find out what happened to the animal.

"Good," I respond. I'm confident, but my voice trembles. The scene around me starts to blur. I feel dizzy. Light-headed. I can barely keep my balance. *Did I hit it? Did I miss?*

Dad jogs farther down the gravel road in search of the bear. He sees something in the slash.

"You got him!"

I can hear the pride in Dad's voice. Hunting a large North American game animal is a big deal, a rite of passage. He runs toward me, arms outstretched. "Holy moly! After all that, you got him! I can't believe it, Eve. Your first bear!" He shakes his head in disbelief that his little dancing queen who, only two years earlier, had zero desire to hunt made a perfect shot under pressure. I'm proud, too, slowly coming out of the haze.

I follow Dad, careful step after careful step, up the hill. The giant stumps, piles of tangled branches, and rotting, slippery logs make for a treacherous obstacle course. It's an ideal setting to suffer a twisted ankle or broken leg. There's so much woody debris crisscrossed high off the ground, we walk for a few feet without actually touching down on the forest floor. While trying to balance on a decaying piece of wood, I strain my head forward and to the side. But I can't catch a glimpse of black fur amid the piles of timber ahead of us. Nothing yet.

We trudge along until Dad yells out, "He's right here! And he's beautiful!"

"I'm almost there!" I yell, hopping over a small pile of

brush as I catch sight of a tuft of black hair up ahead. And then I reach my destination.

This extraordinary creature, easily four hundred pounds, lies on the forest floor in eternal slumber. I drop to my knees and sigh, awestruck. "He's magnificent!"

I run my hands through the bear's beautiful and shiny fur coat, then graze my fingers along the length of one of his four-inch claws. His ears show faint teeth marks, and across his face are several white slits, scars, remnants of the many brawls he must have fought over his lifetime. My hand resting gently on his back, I'm overcome with emotion. I'd seen plenty of bears in photos, on television, and as taxidermy mounts, many of these in Dad's office. But this is the first time I've ever been this close to one. I feel proud, but not in an arrogant way. My mouth waters just thinking of the bear stew our cook will whip up when we get back to camp. I think about those living in the local battered-women's shelter where we will donate most of the meat, the months of lunches and dinners this bear will provide them and their children.

And then it hits me. We can't just leave the bear here. We can barely maneuver on foot with just our body weight. How on earth are we supposed to move him down to the truck?

Sometimes on hunts, you get lucky and harvest an animal close enough to a road where you can load it onto your vehicle and transport it to a convenient and suitable area to skin and dress. But in this case, it's impossible. We have no choice but to skin and dress the bear in the middle of the logging slash. Because bears are big animals, this isn't an uncommon practice. Many harvested bears come back to the camp's skinning shed having already been skinned, gutted, and partially cut up. The remaining uncut meat is then ready to be expertly handled by our camp butcher.

As quickly and as safely as possible, Dad, Matt the cameraman, and I hike back to the truck, which is preloaded with field-dressing equipment. On the way, we make mental notes based on terrain markers of where the dead bear is and the best path to return to it. Stepping cautiously over thin logs that roll back and forth with every step, I clutch my gun. It's locked and loaded, safety on, ready in case another bear gets curious. At the truck, we load our arms with Havalon knives, rubber gloves, garbage bags to organize the different cuts of meat and keep them clean, large plastic storage bins to haul the meat back to the truck, water to keep our gloved hands and the meat dirt-free, and a camera to preserve the memory of this unforgettable hunt.

By the way, here's the thing about taking pictures of harvested animals. The way I, and other ethical hunters, see it, the photograph is about respect. We don't treat an animal like a trophy, standing over the elk, deer, moose, or bear with a boastful I-win-you-lose smile. We are paying homage. I'm photographed with an animal to honor it, to recognize that it gave its life for food and sustenance, whether for my family and me, a village in the African bush, or a local organization in need of food donations.

The picture is a keepsake. It reminds me for years to come of the memories made and challenges faced on a hunt. It's a way to preserve the tradition of storytelling for future generations. To share what took place prior to the harvest—the hours practicing shooting, the lessons learned, the steep mountains hiked, the valleys crawled through, the fresh air inhaled, the countless midnight stars stretched above, the glorious sunrises, the captivating nature of the wild. It's the same reason we take pictures of our kids, of bursting through the finish line of a 10K, of holding a diploma and throwing a cap into the air. We worked hard, and we made it. When Dad snaps the photo of me with that bear, I swell with pride. No one can take that moment away from me.

Carrying all the equipment, it takes almost twice as long to get back to the bear. After dropping some bins and a backpack a few feet away, I help clear rocks and branches from an eight-foot-square area. Then comes the bigger task. Dad, sheathed knife in hand, points to me and instructs, "Grab a leg." To Matt he says, "You grab the opposite one." We turn the bear onto its back, limbs pointing toward the sky. Skinning an animal in a shed or an otherwise sanitary environment on a relatively flat surface is not the easiest job in the world; skinning one outdoors amid twigs, leaves, dirt, and myriad insects makes the task even harder. We do everything in our power to keep every inch of meat clean.

As Matt secures the bear's hind legs and I the front, Dad kneels over the animal. With a sharp knife, he makes a long cut through the hide near the breastbone and opens up the bear's abdominal cavity.

Almost two hours later, we hike back down to the truck. Carrying far more weight than what we started with, we struggle with each step over the unstable slash. Lugging a backpack bulging with bear hide and skull forces me to activate core muscles I never knew existed. It takes a few trips to cart bin after bin and bag after bag of bear meat down to the truck. Finally, only backbone, ribs, and guts remain in the slash, waiting to be finished off by bald eagles, ravens, and other scavengers.

I can't stop smiling as we drive back to camp. It's my turn to share my adventure during dinner.

I learned a lot during that trip. By the end of the bear hunt, I took responsibility for setting up the shooting sticks and making sure I was completely ready before I took a shot. Knowing what I needed to do and practicing that more and more as opportunities popped up, I gained more confidence. I was certainly not an expert hunter by the time I headed back to the city, but my mistakes had taught me plenty.

Everyone who has ever been great at something has had to start from the beginning and work her or his way up. Hunting is no different. It's always a challenge to be the new kid on the block, to stand out awkwardly, when we don't know what we're doing. It's not easy to force ourselves to be that vulnerable. It's not easy to step outside our comfort zone and put ourselves in situations we know little about. It won't ever be easy. We will make mistakes, and people may judge us. But if we always opt to keep things comfortable, we won't be challenged. We won't stretch. We won't improve. We won't get better. And we definitely won't grow.

6

HOLDING YOUR OWN

Be strong and courageous. Do not be afraid or discouraged,
for the Lord your God will be with you wherever you go.

—JOSHUA 1:9

ATKA ISLAND, ALASKA, 2011
››

The tiny plane veers, rights itself, then plunges sickeningly
toward a narrow landing strip on Atka, a remote dot of land
in the Aleutian Island chain that sweeps a thousand miles
south and west from the southernmost tip of Alaska. During our flight we have battled unrelenting turbulence, the
gusty winds rushing sideways across the unforgiving Bering
Sea. I'm convinced a landing isn't possible—the wreckage of
failed attempts line several of the landing strips. But then, our
pilot is a pro.

We hit the gravel with such terrible force that I fly out
of my seat several inches before the seat belt yanks me back
down. We hear what sounds like crushing metal. "What
the—" I exclaim. "There's no way this plane didn't just
break!"

Mary, the client sitting next to me, lets out a faint shriek, clutching her bag to her chest. She's well known in our industry, a pro who runs an important hunting magazine. (Think food critic of the hunting world.) Let's just say we are all banking on a positive expedition.

The plane lurches down the strip as the pilot struggles to maintain control. Dan Goodenow, my boss for about two years now, stretches his arms high above his head, uncramping his limbs. He's pretending to be calm. "Welcome to the Aleutian Islands," he says.

We are all alive, and the plane is intact. So . . . amen to that!

Unfortunately, this week-long trip in October 2011 to hunt reindeer has already started out on a sour note. Our original destination was Umnak, a large Aleutian island of rolling hills and valleys and—best of all—a comfortable lodge. But when we landed in Anchorage, Dan discovered a glitch. Somehow the lines of communication had gotten crossed. The Alaskan outfit that had set up our visit told us we were actually headed much farther out the island chain, to remote Atka.

There was no room to make demands. And, at this point, going home wasn't an option. We decided to make the best of the situation.

A few months earlier, in the beginning of summer 2011, Dan had talked to Dad and me about a promo piece he wanted to do about reindeer in an Alaskan hunting territory we represented. Reindeer on the Aleutian Islands have arguably the biggest antlers compared to body size of any North American big-game animal. Closely related to the more common caribou of North America, reindeer were introduced from Siberia to the Aleutian Islands in the early 1900s as a food source for local villagers. Today, they roam freely on several of these volcanic islands.

Reindeer are designed to live on the tundra. Their noses warm the air they breathe before it enters their lungs. The pads on their hooves accommodate different seasons. In the summer, they become like sponges and offer extra traction on soft tundra. In the winter, the pads shrink and tighten. This allows the edges of their hooves to cut into snow and ice, making it easier to travel in cold weather.

We all agreed that the trip here was a golden opportunity for me to host the show on my own and help the company out by accompanying Dan and an important client here. I'd been hunting for about two years by then, accumulating diverse experiences. I'd been back to South Africa, where I hosted the show for the first time and hunted on the veld (open country in southern Africa) for antelope—waterbuck, impala, and kudu. I had also traveled to Quebec's Anticosti Island for white-tailed deer, Newfoundland for moose, Vancouver Island for bear, Colorado for elk, and the Yukon for caribou.

So I was ready for this by now, but Dan was nervous. It probably didn't help that Dad, with a mix of gravity and humor, had warned him, "Your job is to keep Eva safe." Of course my father had full confidence in Dan, but on the plane ride Dan had joked, "Please don't fall off a cliff, or your dad will kill me!"

I promised I wouldn't.

On the 8.7-square-mile, volcanic island of Atka, population 61, thousands of reindeer roam the steep, grassy terrain. Seals and sea lions swim the deep harbors. The temperature when we land is in the forties, but the twenty-mile-per-hour winds make it feel colder.

Joe, our guide on this trip and a former crewman on one of the fishing boats featured on the hit TV show *Deadliest Catch,* is waiting at the airstrip for the three of us when we land. "Great to meet you, Joe," I say, offering a firm handshake. "It's always a good sign when there's an old plane wreck beside the runway, right?"

Standing beside Joe is his assistant, Jimmy. Poker-faced, he just stands there, swallowed up by a Windbreaker three sizes too big.

The two men take us to the main hunting camp. The old, unoccupied house is a bit unconventional. With its linoleum flooring, mustard-yellow couches, and thick, plaid curtains, it seems frozen in the 1970s. In the kitchen that night, over a ten-dollar canned dinner we picked up in Anchorage, the five of us pore over our plans for the next day.

"Mary will be the first hunter up," Joe advises, sipping some soda. "And if there's more than one mature bull in the herd, Eva, you'll be up next."

Dipping a spoon into a bowl of baked beans, I ask, "How far away are the reindeer?

"The herd generally stays put on one end of the island. Takes about four hours on ATVs to get as close as we can on wheels. Then we'll hike to high ground and glass the valleys and hillsides to find the biggest, oldest reindeer bull."

I nod, passing Dan the bread. "Sounds good. What time do we head out in the morning?"

"Six sharp."

I fall asleep that night with reindeer dancing like sugar-plum fairies in my head.

› › ›

In the morning, we load up our all-terrain vehicle with two rifles, one for me and one for Mary, backpacks, some tarps, and a couple of two-person tents, just in case we get stuck and need to hunker down in the wild for a while. Rain drizzles from the black sky, and the wind whips loose strands of hair into my eyes. Dan and Jimmy each ride on their own quads. Joe drives the client and me in a larger ATV that has a roll bar and a bench seat that barely fits the three of us.

Almost immediately, the terrain shows its true colors. I struggle to stay planted on the seat as the ground slopes into one steep ditch after another. At the first one, we nose-dive, ramming the dirt with the front bumper. Joe slams his foot on the gas to kick the back wheels into gear, and we boot up the other side. We just have to hang on.

Once day breaks, a light fog is visible. As is the full picture of the surrounding topography. The landscape seems to rise in a succession of grassy hills, each one higher than the last. Large rocks break the surface. To make progress, Joe keeps downshifting and hitting the gas. "Hold on, girls," he says over the revved-up engine. We lurch forward, whacking into one another with every turn. Stuck in between Joe and the client, I try to find something to grab hold of to keep my balance. Nothing. My body flops around like a rag doll. The ATV shoots over one peak, only to nose-dive down the other side.

"I'm so sorry, Mary," I say over and over again. I'm slamming into her every few seconds. "No worries," she assures me, her voice shaky. "Glad I have a bar to hold on to. I almost got thrown out of this thing!"

By the time the ATV rambles back to level ground, my face is wet from sweat dripping down my temples. My gut instinct signals an alert: *This is not good. There's got to be another way over these hills.* But Joe is the guide, the one who knows this craggy land, so we defer to his judgment despite our gut instincts. *Surely the rest of the ride won't be this vicious.*

Wrong.

We gain altitude via half a dozen dangerous ascents intermingled with deep plunges. The early-morning drizzle turns into a downpour. I can barely see a few feet in front of me through the fog and rain.

Joe slows down. "We've got to wait this out," he finally says, wiping the rain out of his eyes. This is typical when you're hunting in the Aleutians. When booking a trip there, you always have to add a margin of time—an extra few hours or even days—for the inevitable battle with the elements.

For two hours, the five of us huddle up under a tarp canopy we've stretched out over the open vehicles. As thick raindrops pelt rhythmically overhead, the tundra that surrounds us on all sides transforms into wet muck. To pass the time, we talk about the upcoming adventure.

"These hills are freaking me out! Feels like I'm sprouting gray hairs by the minute from the stress!" I remark.

Dan nods. "I've done this hunt a handful of times over the last few years," he says, "but it does seem worse than usual. Maybe because of all the rain and mud." He turns to Joe. "Buddy, it's hard to get traction out there. Maybe there's an easier route we can take? Something that's not so steep?"

Joe tells us there is no easier way to go. He seems confident and assures us that he's been doing this for years and that he knows the terrain and what the vehicles can do. When the rain lets up, we resume our climb. Sandwiched between guide and client and not wanting to keep ramming my elbow into Joe's ribs and hitting Mary with my body, I ask Joe what I should have asked earlier: "Is there a seat belt or something I can use?"

"Yeah," he replies, only half paying attention. "I think there is one, but no one's ever used it."

While the cross strap is easy to see, the lap strap is stuck deep in the back edge of the seat. We dig it out and Joe helps strap me in. "Another question," I ask, pointing to the roll bar. "Will this actually work if the ATV flips back or rolls?

Joe laughs, hands gripping the steering wheel. "I think so. But then again, we've never tried it out."

"Hope we never will."

My stomach churns as Joe guns the ATV up the face of a hill that is now mostly mud. We plunge down the other side too fast for comfort, bouncing over rocks camouflaged under the green and muddy surface. Then, maybe a hundred feet away, another hill looms. The steepest one yet, this one's a monster.

I shake my head. The practically vertical ascent stares us down, menacingly. *This is not good.* Everything in me screams, *No! Don't do it!* Here's a good rule of thumb: If you're on an ATV and come to a hill that looks too steep to climb, it probably is. Go around it.

We park the vehicles. Ahead of us and slightly to the right is a grassy slope. Behind us, hills already conquered. To the left, a thirty-foot drop-off.

"The way I see it," I pipe up, "we have two options. We can go up and over the hill or go around it. I say we go around it."

Joe is confident the vehicles can handle it.

Dan eyes the hill. He pauses before respectfully disagreeing with the guide. "Why don't you let the girls out, Joe? They can hike up the hill, and you can meet them at the top."

The problem, Joe explains, is that he needs our weight in the vehicle to get it up the hill.

I don't buy his logic, but I don't dwell on the thought long. I'm not the guide, and when you're on hunts as the client, you're supposed to respect the leadership. Push aside your preferences. Defer to and trust the person in charge. Still, I feel conflicted. Our company has five rules: *Safety. Safety. Safety. Safety. Safety.* My dad always told me that what matters most at the end of the day is everyone getting home intact. I've been with him in a handful of situations where he backed off from doing something that could have saved him time or resulted in a big reward but that also carried a risk that just wasn't worth it.

While I don't think going up the hill is a great idea, I'm young and a relatively new hunter, and I don't have past experience in these conditions to back it up. And since this is my first time venturing out on a hunt without my father, I don't want to come across as disrespectful or whiny.

Dan rubs his temples, the muscles in his face tense. He looks at me and shrugs. We figure it's time to play ball.

The seat belt taut around my lap, I mutter, "God, please keep us safe."

We need to gain traction—and fast. Without steady momentum up that hill, we will never make it to the top. Trying to find a balance between giving so much throttle that the front of the ATV kicks up and over, and not enough throttle to give us the momentum to keep climbing, Joe starts rumbling up the hill at a reasonable ten miles an hour. Fifty yards, still easing our way up. Another fifty. The muddy ground squishes and splatters under the tires as we scale the height. I turn back and see Dan. He sits on his quad at the base of the hill, watching us ascend.

One part of my mind delivers a warning: *This is not good. This is not good.* The other spits out reassurances: *Calm down, Eva. Joe's got this. He knows what he's doing. He's got this.* The voices rage while the ATV powers forward almost straight up. I feel like an astronaut glued to the seat back of the spacecraft as it lifts off vertically into the sky.

Around a hundred and fifty yards up the face of the hill, Joe slams on the gas full throttle. I jerk around to look at him just as he starts yelling expletives. Dread pours through my veins.

He does not have this! He does not have this!

In a second, maybe even less, the ATV shoots backward, rear end first, like a missile, flying down the hill, wheels barely touching the surface. There is no time to think. No time to grab hold of something. No time to do anything other than scream. Mary joins in. A few colorful words fly out of my mouth as I close my eyes and think: *This is it. Today is the day I am going to die.*

We are headed straight toward the assistant guide, who has been watching the scene from his parked quad at the foot of the hill. The weight of the vehicle and the three of us is sure to crush him. In a split second Jimmy dives headfirst onto the wet ground just a few feet out of the way as we plummet past him, our screams blasting through the open air. The back end of our vehicle smashes into his. But it doesn't stop. Momentum pushes us right over the top of his ATV and over the other side and right toward the thirty-foot drop-off. Then it happens. At breakneck speed, we catapult backward off the cliff. I close my eyes, duck my head into my lap, and pray. I don't know it at the time, but as we free-fall, Joe, unrestrained, is hurled out of the vehicle, his body slamming onto the jagged rocks below with bone-crushing force.

The ATV crashes into the earth at the bottom of the cliff, back end first, but then starts tumbling sideways. Side over side we roll until the vehicle finally teeters slowly back and forth like a spinning penny on its last few rotations. Then the

ATV is motionless, resting on the driver's side. I'm still alive. Heart racing, I open my eyes.

The seat belt suspends me in midair. My arms and legs dangle awkwardly. An eerie silence surrounds us. My vision blurs, and my breath is ragged. It occurs to me, *We had an accident. We flew off the hill and crashed.*

I can hear someone moaning, but it's hard to tell where the sound is coming from.

Where's Mary?

Where's Joe?

Is anyone dead?

Am I hurt?

Am I dead?

Mary is lying on the ground below me, her torso visible through the driver's side opening. *Where's the rest of her?* Blinking a few times to clear the blurriness, I notice that the other half of her body is pinned under the vehicle. I swallow hard, hands trembling from fear of the unknown. *Oh, my gosh. Is she okay?* As I gape in horror at her still body, I hear a man's voice. The sound is faint, dulled by my shock.

"Eva! Eva! I'm coming!"

The voice sounds familiar. *Dan,* I finally realize, slowly coming back into the reality of the moment.

In a dreamlike haze, I watch Dan scrambling and sliding toward us down the rocky slope. When he gets to our vehicle, I smile weakly and tell him I'm fine. Despite the dull ache that wraps my body, nothing feels broken, and I don't see blood.

Dan carefully unbuckles me out of the vehicle, tears in

his eyes, repeating over and over, "I'm so sorry, Eva. I'm so sorry."

"Stop," I say, my voice hoarse. "I'm fine, Dan. It's not your fault." There's no time to exchange reassurances or apologies. We have to get the client out. Dan calls to Mary.

She responds, her voice trembling. "I'm here. I'm alive. I think I'm okay."

With brute strength likely boosted by sheer adrenaline, Dan and a mud-covered Jimmy flip the quad right-side up. Mary looks dazed, and she clutches her neck, wincing in pain.

I panic. "Where's Joe?"

A few moments later, we find him moaning against the cliff face. Some of his fingers are broken, contorted at grotesque angles. Probably his ribs, too, as he doubles up in agony.

Dan takes charge, and his calm manner is a blessing. Panic usually only makes things worse.

The crash has deposited our belongings all over the place. To the left, a tarp. To the right, some sleeping bags. Up ahead, a tent. Trembling, Mary and I pitch in to gather up the scattered items.

When I locate the bulky satellite phone, I punch in the numbers of the hunting lodge. Nothing. The battery is dead; poor preparation on our part. There's no way to call for help. My mind cloudy, I sling someone's muddy backpack over my shoulder and notice the camera bag a few feet away.

"The show," I gasp. My instinct is to start filming. It's the unexpected moments in a hunt that create great television, and I don't want to leave this place without footage. But, still in shock, I can't comprehend that our hunting trip is likely over.

I sweep the camera in every direction. Through the lens, the mangled vehicles appear, and my hunting companions, their faces white. Walking zombies. I clear my throat, the noise almost deafening in the haunting silence. "We just . . . we just went flying down the mountain," I begin recording. Someone asks me to turn off the camera.

I comply. *But what about the show?* I think. But, really, there's no point to keep filming. There's nothing to show but a shaken hunting party and a whole lot of mud. We need to get home. Or at least back to civilization.

Despite the scratches, crushed plastic, and bent metal, the vehicles carry us on the four-hour drive back to camp. My heart is stuck in my throat as we roll forward, particularly when we face the first circuit of threatening hills. The first few are manageable. I try to prop Mary up, absorbing as much bouncing as I can on her behalf. When we reach a hill that looks too steep, I turn to Joe. Black circles shadow his eyes, his left arm clamped tightly around his chest. "Mary and I are walking," I tell him firmly, not wanting to test fate. "We'll see you on the other side."

By 6:00 p.m., we roll into the village, a miserable picture of bruised spirits, mud-drenched clothes, and broken bones bouncing along in half-wrecked chariots. Driving rain as thick as a wall has just begun to fall, coupled with violent gusts of wind. Mother Nature shakes her finger at us. *You're not going anywhere anytime soon.* Crouched over in pain, Joe can barely stand up. Mary's not faring so well, either. They both need immediate medical attention.

We meet up with the village health aide, the only medical support on this remote island. Though this woman has only minimal medical training, she does have twenty-four-hour telephone access to a doctor at an Anchorage hospital who can diagnose more serious injuries and conditions. Over the phone that hospital physician diagnoses Joe with broken fingers and ribs and Mary with a severe case of whiplash. He also prescribes painkillers, giving the health aide the code to the locked safe on the island where narcotics are stored and doled out only in medical emergencies.

When we finally get back to the house, it's time to call home. My fingers shake violently as I dial Mom's number. She answers on the second ring. "Hello?" Her voice is melodic.

Shoulders shaking, I erupt in sobs. "M-m-mom!" For a minute or two I just cry, barely hearing anything she's saying.

"Honey? What's wrong? Are you all right?"

I begin to contain myself and force a sniffle back. "Mom, we're okay. But we've—we've been in an accident." The sobs resume, my tears contagious. Mom starts crying, the first few minutes of our conversation filled with more crying than words.

The rest of the evening is a blur. Dan, Mary, and I have dinner before going to bed. Not that anyone eats. We push a few beans around with our spoons. "I'm sorry, Eva. I really am," Dan says. "I never should have let that happen. I knew it was a bad idea. And I just stood there and watched. I am so, so sorry. Forgive me for not protecting you."

I feel guilty for his heartfelt remorse. "It's not your fault. Oh, my goodness, it's not. This was an accident. I just can't believe we all walked away relatively unscathed."

The steel frame of the bed I crawl into that night squeaks loudly. Pulling the thin sheets, threadbare in spots, up to my neck, I feel waves of regret wash over me. *Why hadn't I trusted my gut instinct?*

I reflect on my life, bringing to mind the number of times I intuitively knew what to do but didn't do it. I think of a past relationship that was, to put it mildly, unhealthy. Though I could see how toxic it was, I stuck it out. I believed that if we broke up, I'd be alone forever. So I forced myself to believe that the relationship was worth staying in. Things only got worse. Eventually, I wised up and left. It took a lot of mistakes along the way, but I finally learned to stay true to myself and pay attention to my gut.

I shiver through my thermal long johns. As homesick as I am, I'm grateful to be alive. And though I can't see Him with my eyes or physically feel His outstretched hand, I know God is with me. Watching over me. There aren't enough ways to say *thank you* for what I'm feeling. *Thank you, God, for keeping me safe. Thank you for keeping everyone else safe. Thank you for not letting this be the last day of my life. Thank you for being there with us. Thank you for helping us get back to safety.* And somewhere, lost in my heartfelt tribute of gratitude, I doze off.

❯ ❯ ❯

I was so glad to make it home the next day, I almost kissed the ground.

If you're wondering, when the three of us sat down for a debrief a few days later, Dad gave both Dan and me quite an earful. "Did you not remember the five rules we have?" he fumed. From that hunt onward, those five words were ingrained forever in my mind.

Hunting in remote areas is inherently dangerous. These adventures into the world's most wild lands always involve risks, and every guide and hunter has a different comfort level with what chances to take. Nine times out of ten, going up a steep hill soaked in mud might turn out okay. In our case, it didn't. Even the most seasoned wilderness guide, with safety top of mind, can make a misstep. This is part of a life spent outdoors. Accidents will happen. Still, we strive to do our best to avoid them.

On that trip, I learned the hard way that you don't have to be the most experienced to have good instincts. Even an outsider embarking on a new adventure can recognize warning signs or sense trouble, and maybe having a fresh perspective is actually an advantage. Sometimes it can bring clarity, an uncluttered viewpoint free of bias. Clearly, Joe knew what he was doing. And he had a wealth of experience to back it up. But sometimes even the most experienced of us can benefit when we stop, pause, and reassess a situation through a new lens.

While that hunting trip culminated in an ending that was unexpected and quite traumatic, I didn't consider giving up on solo trips. A big part of why I love hunting is the adventure and the challenges that come with it. And my love for the lifestyle would not evolve full circle if I stepped back from every danger. I'd only cheat myself out of opportunities to grow, as a hunter and as an individual. I had no choice but to keep going. Even if it meant facing my fears.

Problem was, I was the only one who felt that way. As hard as I tried to convince Dad and Dan to sign me up for another solo hunt, the two kept brushing me off. Not one to back down, I hounded them for almost two years. Finally, I got my chance.

In spring 2013, I caught Dan at just the right moment. He was in the process of booking hunts, and I noticed he had an opening in August—a reindeer hunt on the Aleutian Islands.

"How about scheduling me in?" I offered with a sugary-sweet smile. "And here's a great idea. How about we do something different and turn it into an all-girls hunting trip?"

Dan's stony face perked up. "Now, that's a thought. But are you sure you want to go back there?"

"Are you kidding? It's time to finish what we started."

Dan got on board. Dad, too . . . eventually.

For this trip, I brought along my friend Rachelle, a tall blonde from West Virginia who can disarm anyone with her sweet and sincere personality. Her dad, an avid hunter, died of cancer when she was only seven, so she never got the chance to hunt with him. Rather, Rachelle started hunting when she met her husband, an outfitter, and she immediately fell in love with the lifestyle. I also invited Taylor, a young woman with an infectious personality and gorgeous curly hair. I met her at a precision-shooting class years back. Though her dad was a client of ours and hunted all over the world, she was fairly new to the lifestyle.

The three of us flew into the village of Nikolski, population 18, on the island of Umnak, the third largest island in the Aleutian archipelago. From the start of the trip, the vibe was way different from that of my excursion two years earlier. There's a stark contrast between hunting with an all-male crew and hunting with your girlfriends. Oh, we were just as serious and hard-core when we needed to be, but when we didn't, there was a lot more laughing involved. Needless to say, the entire trip was a blast, even though we battled a nonstop wind that made the otherwise forty-something-degree weather feel freezing.

A two-hour, bumpy-as-expected ride on two ATVs brought us to some gently sloping valleys and grassy rolling hills. I'll admit, hopping back into the same type of ATV I had crashed in two years earlier brought about the beginnings of a panic attack. I had to talk myself down hysteria lane while we jostled along. It sure helped, though, that, while some of the hills were steep, they were moguls compared to the ones on Atka.

When we made our way into reindeer territory, the scenic picture took my breath away. Broad valleys spread out in a blanket of lush ferns. Tall grass swayed rhythmically in the wind. In the distance, snowcapped mountains, one an active volcano, stood guard over the land below. And feeding on alpine moss and tall grass, hundreds upon hundreds of reindeer gathered, their large, smooth, white antlers glinting in the summer sun.

On foot, the three of us, along with the guide, crept quietly through the valley, crouched low. Rachelle hunted first. After crawling on hands and knees to get closer to the animals we'd seen, then glassing to find a bull, we noticed huge antlers in the distance, unmoving and low to the ground. Likely a napping bull, about five hundred yards away. As we closed the distance to two hundred yards, we saw that we were right. We inched even closer. Finally, the bull stood up. When he turned broadside, Rachelle took the shot, harvesting her first reindeer. Two days later, Taylor and I harvested mature bulls within a hundred yards of each other on a marshy hillside, with Rachelle there to share the excitement.

Our girls' expedition ended on a high note. For the first time, I discovered the unique camaraderie that can unfold with other women in an otherwise male-dominated field. This marked a turning point in my life. I wanted to proclaim to the world that it was great to be a female hunter, that we weren't alone, and that there must be many others like us out there.

It's amazing what happens when we face our fears head-on. Opportunities open up. Doors swing open. We find ourselves doing wonderful things that we would have missed had we submitted to our fears. I often think of those experiences in my life that never would have happened had I given up somewhere along the way. If the Atka accident had scared me enough to quit hunting back in 2011, I never would have traveled to Raleigh, North Carolina, a year later, to the hunting expo where I met my future husband. I never would have seen the Northern Lights shining brightly above our campfire in the Yukon. I never would have ventured to New Zealand, Argentina, Spain, and France to hunt some of the most magnificent animals on earth. I never would have embraced the possibilities that streamed under the surface of the unknown, waiting to push through and enter the realm of existence.

7

ONE CLEAN SHOT

Now then, get your equipment—your quiver and bow—
and go out to the open country to hunt some
wild game for me.

—GENESIS 27:3

MAGNITOGORSK, RUSSIA, 2014

"*Field & Stream* would like you to be on the cover of their
May issue, themed 'What's Next?' Are you interested?"

My jaw drops nearly to the floor. I read the e-mail again.
And again. And a few more times after that.

Oh. My. Goodness. We're talking about the world's leading outdoor magazine. The authority on fishing and hunting
with one million subscribers and more than two million online visitors per month. The glossy pages I had seen plastered
on practically every tabletop in our house growing up. *Interested? Are you kidding??*

"No way!" I say aloud to no one.

By this point, I've been hunting for five years and co-
hosting the show with Dad, but I'm only one of many young
women who love to hunt. The only other female who has
ever graced the front cover of *Field & Stream* was Queen

Elizabeth, almost forty years earlier. On the January 1976 edition, Her Royal Highness was pictured wearing a dainty red sweater and a knee-length plaid skirt on the castle lawn, along with four of her hunting dogs. So to follow *her*—*that* seems insane!

When *Field & Stream* comes calling, it's February 2014. For reasons I'll get to shortly, I'm living in Magnitogorsk, an industrial city in Russia. Magnitogorsk is drab. Located nine hundred miles southeast of Moscow, it's home to the largest iron and steel works in the country. Everywhere I look, I see flat gray or dull brown, in the form of a wall to a neighboring building, even the sky at times. In a climate with an average winter temperature of below zero and frequent downpours of freezing rain and snow, I'm stuck indoors most days. And, no, I'm not here to hunt.

Let's pause for a minute. You know what this story is missing so far? Romance. Most good tales involve something that at least resembles a love story. I think it's time to tell mine. Because only falling in love could convince me to live in a city hailed as the "steel heart of the Motherland" where almost no one spoke English.

Two years earlier, in March 2012, I held a meet-and-greet at the Dixie Deer Classic, a three-day trade show for hunters and fishermen in Raleigh, North Carolina. A scruffy-faced, baseball-cap-wearing cutie, six feet tall and gorgeous, introduced himself. "Hi, I'm Tim," he said. He then pointed to his buddy, "This is my friend Greg. I hear you're from Canada."

"Nice to meet you, Tim. And, yes, I'm from the West

Coast, near Vancouver." I turned to his friend. "Nice to meet you, too, Greg."

"I gotta say, it's really nice to hear a Canadian accent. Everyone around here has such a strong southern one," Tim said with a twinkle in his eye.

Nodding, I laugh. "So, what brings you out here to Raleigh?"

"I've been working here."

"Cool. What do you do?"

"I play hockey for a local team." I appreciated the modesty, but as a Canadian, I was familiar with how the sport of hockey worked. The only "local" hockey team in Raleigh was the professional one: the NHL's Carolina Hurricanes. Tim seemed like a pretty humble guy. I liked that. Over the next few minutes, we talked more, mainly about hunting and fishing. I learned that these were two of his favorite pastimes. And, well, that was that.

A few months later, I opened a private message on Twitter. "Hey, Eva, not sure if you remember me, but we met in Raleigh at the Dixie Deer Classic. Just wanted to say hi and see how your fall is going." *Um, yes, I remember you, Tim!* That message led to a six-month private conversation over Twitter that eventually graduated to e-mail. Tim and I checked in with each other every few weeks. I was busy and on the road a lot. I wasn't looking for, nor did I have time for, a beau. And, frankly, I liked the single life. All I had to think about was me and my next adventure.

That said, many things about Tim caught my attention, even though I barely knew him and we lived across the

127

continent from each other. He was sweet and kind. He loved the outdoors and his family. He asked questions and seemed interested in the answers. He was smart and knew what he wanted. Looking back, I find it ironic that Grandpa Len (who was a hockey player himself and a bit of a ladies' man) always advised me to "never marry a hockey player." This seemed like a good suggestion, based on some of the rough-around-the-edges guys he'd played with growing up. But Tim was different. After some heavy Google-stalking action, I learned that he had recently donated his Harley-Davidson motorcycle to a local charity's fund-raiser. I'd never known a guy who would do something like that.

In spring 2013, about a year after we met in Raleigh, Tim and I finally talked on the phone. Tim was the first to say, "I'd really like to see you again."

I couldn't have agreed more, but the problem was, my calendar was blocked in left and right with hunting trips and work events. "I have a six-day opening after an upcoming trip to Wisconsin before a back-to-back cluster of hunts," I offered. But, to be honest, a part of me hoped he wouldn't be available, because the idea of meeting up with him after so long seemed crazy.

Tim was motivated, though. "I can make it work," he said calmly.

Our first date was dinner in downtown Raleigh. I'll never forget that when we left the restaurant, about fifteen college guys were getting off a party bus at the curb. They stared at us for an awkwardly long time, and a few of them started jabbing whoever was close in the ribs with their elbows. Just

Letting the arrow fly. As a little girl I always preferred to dance, but shooting a plastic bow with suction-cup arrows was the first step toward discovering my passion for the great outdoors.

My mother in 1978 in the Montréal, Quebec, studio where she taught dance. This woman has the most poise, grace, and beauty of anyone I've ever known.

Two years old with big dreams to one day become a ballerina. Man plans and God laughs!

Settling into camp on one of our many Shockey family "vacations," a.k.a. "hunting trips in disguise." Here's Dad, Bran, and me in northern British Columbia.

The Shockeys on safari in Tanzania in 2002. Stepping away from my comfort zone of summer fun with friends and finally loving every bit of this amazing adventure.

South Africa, 2009, where my hunting obsession began. First hunt ever and coached by the best—Dad.

Getting ready to hunt for bears on northern Vancouver Island. Fresh air and hunting with your family does the soul good.

Grateful for getting to hunt with the greatest dad on earth, who has shared his passion with me for hunting, the outdoors, and conservation.

Nothing like hunting white-tailed deer with the love of your life. In Saskatchewan, 2014, with my husband (then fiancé), Tim Brent, who was on a break from playing hockey in Russia.

What an incredible experience to launch the first-ever premium Bowtech bow for serious female hunters at the Archery Trade Association expo in 2015.

Getting focused for a bow hunt on Vancouver Island. Let the adventure begin.

Glassing for moose and caribou in the Yukon, God's country. This is as close to heaven on earth as you can get.

When you get to harvest a 1,500-pound moose that will feed all the guests at your wedding, consider it a blessed day. Makes the prep, the achy muscles, the grime, and the hard work all worth it.

Preparing the main dish at my wedding. These juicy slices of meat came from the Alaskan-Yukon moose I harvested in 2014.

Field to table! When you know exactly where your organic wild game meat comes from, nothing tastes better. I'm sure my wedding guests would agree. Bon appétit!

Finally at the top of an 8,000-foot mountain in New Mexico, about to glass for elk. Took a bit longer than I thought. Probably because I was seven-and-a-half months pregnant with my daughter, Leni Bow.

before Tim and I started walking down the street, one of them piped up, "Hey, are you Eva Shockey?" And for the next five minutes, Tim graciously played the role of photographer, snapping pictures of me and these guys with each of their phones. I can't help but think that that impressed my professional-hockey-player date, who was used to being the one recognized in his neck of the woods.

The next day Tim and I took a road trip to explore Charleston, South Carolina. I know. Probably not the best idea to spend a few days driving with a relative stranger. But between what I did know of Tim and the fact that he was a well-known athlete, I figured he had too much at stake to kill me and toss my lifeless body into a ditch somewhere.

Needless to say, he wasn't a murderer. We clicked immediately. By day two of our adventure in the Carolinas, I called my mom. "I'm in big trouble," I said. And by the time Tim flew to British Columbia a few weeks later to meet my parents, I was already in love with him. In the last week of July (only two months after we started dating!), Tim was offered a contract to play for a professional hockey team in Russia. We had a long talk about the future. It ended with Tim's decision: "This is a really great opportunity for my career and to set us up for the future, but I will turn it down if you aren't okay with it. I'm not going without you."

With that, we were Russia-bound! Over the next two years that we spent overseas for hockey, I'd make the long trek back and forth to North America at least once a month for hunting trips (such as the one I talked about in Chapter 6) and various work commitments. Being stuck inside four walls in the steel heart of the Russian Motherland did a number on my sanity, so the trips were a godsend. I would savor every moment I got in the outdoors and marvel at the ways I was becoming more proficient in the art of hunting. My confidence in the field was growing as I learned through experience the best tactics to use in any given hunting situation.

And that all led back to that surprise e-mail in February 2014.

> > >

Fired up, barely able to sit still in our tiny prefabricated Russian apartment, I hit Reply. "Wow! Is this for real?! That's incredible!!" It's hard to stop myself from clicking the exclamation-mark key a dozen times. "Only thing is," I continue, "I'm in Russia and won't be back in the States until next month. Can I do the photo shoot then?"

The reply shows up within twenty-four hours. "We need you here next week."

"Okay, let's do it!" I type, shivering. A blustering wind outside is driving icy snow particles against our single-pane window, already caked in a layer of frost.

I book a flight immediately. Travel to the States takes a minimum of thirty hours with multiple layovers—not to mention major jet lag, since the Big Apple is nine hours behind Magnitogorsk time. But who cares? It's for *Field & Stream*. Seriously, *Field & Stream*!

Instructions are simple. "Bring whatever you would

normally wear on a hunt." Easy enough, except I don't have any hunting clothes in Russia. Somewhere floating around North America en route to my next hunt is my duffle bag packed with pants, shirts, jackets, and a pair of boots from the previous hunt. We reroute the bag to the shoot location, but I realize everything in the bag is dirty and sweaty. I won't get a chance to wash the clothes before the shoot.

Thirty-five hours pass from the time I close my apartment door in Magnitogorsk to the time I arrive on set in the Chelsea neighborhood of Manhattan. In a daze, I stumble out of a yellow taxi, hoping I've counted the correct change. Pushing open the heavy front door of the warehouse where the shoot will take place is like walking into a tsunami of chaos.

About fifteen people are rushing around. A woman is waving a clipboard, yelling at someone through an apparatus dangling from her ear. "I told you to have that here by 9:00 a.m. This is not going to work!" A few guys in black T-shirts, sweat dripping down their faces, haul heavy lighting equipment and cloth backdrops from one side of the room to the other. "Come on, guys, let's get this done!" A couple of people gather around a makeup table, whipping out and meticulously organizing hair products, makeup brushes, and pots and pots of camouflage-colored cosmetics.

Draped in shock as I witness the unfolding of artistic bedlam, I walk slowly through the warehouse. When I see my stinky hunting clothes hanging neatly on an aluminum rack, freshly steamed and pressed, I cringe. *Someone had to actually touch my dirty clothes!*

I'd done a number of photo shoots before, but nothing

with this level of pomp and circumstance. I think it's Art Streiber, the award-winning photographer of high-profile sports and entertainment figures, who notices me first. His smile is disarming.

"Well, Eva," he says, his eyes bright behind his wire-rimmed eyeglasses, "you're the first cover model I've photographed who showed up without an entourage."

I laugh. *Entourage?* Who would I have brought—Dad? "Yup, it's just me."

"Well, let's get started." Art leads me a few feet over to an idea board. "I don't think you've been briefed on our plan. We want the cover to be raw and natural. A natural-born hunter who doesn't look like the traditional version of a hunter."

"I love it!" I respond. Then, after chatting a bit more, I'm whisked away by a hair stylist and makeup artist. While one brushes my hair into a loose side braid, the other scrubs my face clean, barely applying any makeup. A horrifying thought when you're about to face a high-definition camera close-up.

Standing in front of a green backdrop wearing a camo-colored hoodie and pants and holding a new bow Bowtech had just sent to the shoot, I warn Art, "Listen, before we start, I want you to know, I'm a terrible actor. I can be me all day long, but if you want me to pretend to be someone I'm not for these photos, it's going to look weird and awkward, and people will see right through it."

Art nods knowingly. "Don't worry. I got you. Now draw your bow and pretend you're about to shoot an animal." *Click. Flash. Click.*

After I draw back, I realize that no one in the room is familiar with the dangers or safety precautions of hunting weapons. I quickly let down my bow and face the crowd standing around Art. "Okay, hold up a second. You guys need to know that this bow is not a prop. It's a real weapon. And there's no way to fake draw a bow. Once the arrow is nocked and I'm at full draw, the bow will shoot if I accidentally touch the release. So when I'm drawing, everyone has to stand behind me. I know this isn't a hunting environment, but we still have to treat it like one."

The crew members comply, and the photo shoot flies by in a succession of instructions and flashes. Toward the end, the makeup artist streaks my skin with olive and brown face paint. Art continues to guide me with expertise.

"Now hold the bow up on your shoulder. Look gritty." *Click. Flash. Click.*

"Okay, now walk toward me but look past me." *Click. Flash. Click.*

"Look serious." *Click. Flash. Click.*

"Look natural." *Click. Flash. Click.*

"Look tense." *Click. Flash. Click.*

During the shoot, I also film a video segment and answer a few questions. Highlighting how more and more women are participating in the lifestyle, I also explain how hunting is a natural way for me to continue generations of family tradition and spend time with the ones I love. As I talk, I notice a few of the crew nodding their heads as they listen.

The next morning, I'm back on a plane bound for Russia. Before passing out from exhaustion, I stare out the window.

The view of the city that never sleeps slips farther and farther away. *Did that really happen? Was all that talking and photographing really going to show up in the magazine?* It's hard to take in. When I was a little girl, I'd dream of seeing my name in lights, maybe at an opening for a major ballet production or on a sign as the owner of a famous dance school. But never this.

Toward the middle of April, Tim and I are in Prague for a playoff game. The hotel lobby is crammed with bulky hockey players and their families drinking coffee and spitting out fast-paced conversations in Russian. We sit with Chris Lee, one of Tim's teammates from Canada. As I inhale the aromatic brew in my cup, I notice Chris's father emerging from the crowd. He's just arrived from Canada to visit his son. We met once—he's a hunter, too. Instant camaraderie.

After hugging Chris, Mr. Lee reaches into his bag and turns toward me. A big smile spreads over his face. "I heard you've been looking for this," he says, slapping a shiny magazine into my hand.

As I look down, my eyes widen. The magazine almost nose-dives onto the tiled floor. *They did it!* Field & Stream *really put me on the cover!*

Reality finally sinks in. The e-mails, the calls, and the texts I'd gotten over the last several days about the article finally become real. Seeing something for yourself is much different from someone telling you about it. "Wow! Oh, my gosh!" My hands can't stop shaking. Tim wraps his arms around me and says, "I'm so proud of you!" Chris and his dad smile. "Congratulations," they repeat. And thousands upon thousands of miles away from home, standing in the middle of a European hotel lobby, surrounded by people oblivious to the excitement rushing through me, the four of us celebrate.

But, truthfully, the celebration isn't about me. We are applauding a long-respected magazine for taking a leap of faith to recognize the women now participating in a male-dominated field. We are giving props to female hunters identified in the industry as the "next big thing." I feel beyond blessed to be a spokesperson for the many women who've chosen to push through the resistance of stereotypes and create their own adventures.

> > >

Six months later, in November 2014, I walk into the woods of Saskatchewan. White-tailed deer, here I come. My hands hold a Bowtech Carbon Rose, the same bow I was photographed with for *Field & Stream*. It's light and quiet but deadly, and it's much faster than my last bow. The quiver is locked and loaded with five carbon-shaft arrows tipped with razor-sharp fixed-blade broad heads.

I've grown to love whitetail season since my first run four years ago. I breathe deeply. I can't wait to soak in fresh air and witness the flux of creation.

Though I'd been practicing since my first trip to South Africa, I'd only been actively hunting with a compound bow for about three years. In 2013, I made my first harvests with a bow, a bear in the spring and a buck in the fall. Bow hunting can be stressful. The second my gaze lands on animal, I run through each of the steps required to make a good shot. At the same time, my adrenaline activates its overdrive button, and a tangled mesh of emotions explodes. My breath is ragged. And the checklist running through my brain of making sure I have the right body position, the right anchor point, steady hands, control of my breaths, can sometimes grow blurry.

I'm accompanied by Brian "Wojo," one of our company's full-time guides who has been with us since I was a little girl. Tall, with a burly build and a bushy white beard, Wojo looks intimidating. But this expert hunter is really a softie at heart. Tim, now my fiancé, comes along, too. But he spends just the first five days with us before heading back to Russia to continue his second season of hockey. This is his first hunt with me, but he knows the drill. He's hunted whitetail many times in the Midwestern United States and eastern Canada. Used to hunting in a tree stand, this is his first time sitting in a ground blind. It means a lot to share the lifestyle with someone I love and someone who, as I do, desires to pass it down to future generations.

The evening before the hunt, I slide the trail-camera memory cards into my computer. It doesn't take long to see some good footage. "Oooh, there's a nice buck! Look how long his tines are."

Let's break for some deer talk. With rare exceptions, only male deer, or bucks, grow antlers. A buck's antlers generally have two main "beams." A tine is a growth off a main beam. For the most part, if a tine is at least an inch long, it is considered a point. Now, several different scoring systems exist to rate a buck. Some hunters, including those in the United States, will count the tines on a buck's antlers and refer to it by that number. For instance, a buck with eight tines will be referred to as an "eight point." Some hunters split up each side of the rack of antlers. So if a buck has five tines on one side and four on the other, they'd call him a "five by four." Some scoring systems are more elaborate, while some hunters judge animals based solely on weight. It's all a matter of preference, and I find no one method better than the next.

Back to that photo. I linger on the ten-point buck that glares straight into the camera lens. His thick neck and muscular shoulders top a slightly saggy belly, all telltale signs of maturity. Standing tall and proud, this buck is the biggest we've seen on camera on the entire property.

"Yeah," Wojo says, nodding. "That's a wide rack. Definitely a shooter."

Clicking the arrow buttons on the keyboard, I notice more footage of him. "He's standing totally broadside, but mostly at night. This buck's got to be nocturnal. Doesn't look too good for me."

Wojo is unaffected by that fact. "He's going to mess up eventually and come in during the day. I got a feeling you're going to shoot your buck, Eva!"

The longer I stare, the more familiar I find the shape and characteristics of his antlers. "We've seen this buck before, Wojo."

Can you really tell a deer from his antlers? Yes. Let me explain.

Each year male deer grow new sets of antlers. Nourished

by a maze of arteries and veins, antlers are one of the fastest growing tissues on earth. They can grow up to half an inch each day, beginning in the spring and continuing through summer, when they reach completion. As they grow, they are covered with a thin layer of a soft, living membrane called velvet—this falls off when the deer's testosterone level increases and the tissue hardens into bone. Hard antlers stay on through the peak of breeding season. Once the testosterone level begins to dip, the pedicles—the points on the buck's head from which the antlers emerge—will weaken to the point where the antlers simply fall off. This process is repeated year after year.

Unless deer have been injured or are malnourished, their racks will typically grow back in the same unique shape and with the same characteristics, just bigger (or smaller if they're old or their health is deteriorating). Antler growth is typically dependent on the buck's health. For instance, although no one really knows why, injuries that occur to a deer's hind leg can result in deformed antlers, either temporarily or in consecutive years, on the opposite side of the injury.

Taking a second look at that photograph of the massive buck, I tell Wojo, "Yup. I'm pretty sure we got him on camera last year."

"Let's go through the old photos," Wojo suggests. An hour of clicking through last year's footage around this one particular blind, I finally see the same buck. His antlers are slightly smaller but have the same unique frame. It takes hours and intense scrutiny, but we manage to pinpoint this same buck for the past four seasons.

"He's got to be at least six years old," I estimate. "He didn't get that big and old from being dumb, that's for sure." During the last few seasons, this buck was rarely captured on film in daylight. I wasn't optimistic that he'd suddenly change his habits and show up during our sits.

Thankfully, Wojo didn't share my sentiment. "Let's give it a shot! Let's find your buck!"

We're hunting early in the season, before the rut, which offers more predictable deer activity. Gauging their behavior is not an exact science, since they're wild animals, but it's possible to spot patterns. Generally speaking, deer movement during this time of year happens early in the morning until around 11:00 a.m. The next few hours are pretty quiet, so we normally return to the house and check the memory cards from the other cameras around the property. We then head back to the blind in the midafternoon, when deer activity picks up again.

Day one is unseasonably warm. Wearing a fleece zip-up that would, over the next few hours, prove too hot, I step into a ground blind. It wasn't my first choice. I'd hoped to sit in the blind where the most deer activity was captured on film, but the wind wasn't in our favor there. This six-foot-deep hole is covered on the outside with a plexus of leaf-free branches and twigs. The inside dirt walls are moist, speckled with hay. The blind's opening is veiled mostly by camo mesh. The space is tight. Just enough room to accommodate Wojo, Tim, the cameraman, and me. A tall mound of packed dirt sits in a corner, a makeshift bench.

Thirty minutes before sunrise, the official start time to

hunt, I'm on my feet, leaning on the front wall of the blind. Eyes glued to a pair of binoculars, I peer through the opening and wish I had the superhuman power to see through tangible objects. Such as the thicket of trees before me. My bow waits for the call to action, hung from a steel hook at the top of the blind.

This day, I see nothing but the occasional magpie flapping around and a handful of manic squirrels. Toward the end of the second sitting, my stomach starts rumbling. I reach into my pants pocket for a snack. My fingers stumble upon a pile of gummy goop from some candy last season. *Gross!* (There's a running joke in our company about what snacks I leave behind where and who will find them. Someone should start putting money on those bets.)

Day one is a bust. We may have seen a doe or two, but that's about it. The lack of deer movement is definitely due to the unseasonably warm weather. I bet most of the bucks are holed up until dark, when the temperature will drop. I'm not worried, though. It's only the first day.

On day two, we get skunked again. Same on days three to five, when we switch to a pop-up blind. "Where are the bucks?" I groan as Tim packs up to return to Russia before we've even had a chance at a buck.

"They'll come," he assures me. "We're just having bad luck with this weather."

"This is annoying. Where is that cold front? The more time that passes, the more anxious I get."

I hate wrestling with this feeling. And though I know deer movement and patterns are beyond my control, I'm still responsible to produce a great TV show. And at this point, in the absence of action, it's pretty boring. I do not want to go home knowing I hosted a snooze-fest.

But instead of allowing the pressure to toy with my emotions and dampen my confidence, I do what I always do in such moments. I practice shooting my bow behind the farmhouse. Squaring up in position, I face the Block Target. Riddled with holes and tears from hours and hours of practice over the years, it's a well-worn and welcoming sight. As the wind whistles through the tall grass, I draw my bow release back to my cheek. The string is taut against the tip of my nose. As I slowly unleash the arrow, the spinning practice blade torpedoes right into the target with a thump. My tension subsides.

On day eight, we leave the house, warming immediately in the mild temperature. I could have hunted all day in a T-shirt and been comfortable. While that wasn't the best news for our hunt, I am armed with some good news. The wind has finally changed directions, which means a cold front is likely blowing in.

As I set up shop inside the blind that afternoon, I turn to Wojo. "I've got to say, it feels so much better to get a whitetail when you've worked for it than if it just walks out on the first day."

"Isn't that the truth!" he says, nodding.

"But that wouldn't have been so bad, either!"

As dusk approaches, a smattering of bucks amble past the blind.

"Get ready, Eva," Wojo whispers, his voice tense with excitement.

I watch the thick bodies loiter about. They graze a bit and keep walking. Suddenly, my eyes catch a glimpse of a larger buck. I strain my head forward to get a closer look. *It's him! It's gotta be! Same wide rack. Same Roman nose. He's not nocturnal after all!* My adrenaline starts pumping as I try to absorb the approach of the mysterious buck. He comes as close as forty yards, a distance I'd practiced on a target. As I grip my bow, my mind races. I had committed to shooting no more than twenty-five yards away, but his presence so late in our trip makes me want to change my mind. In a split second, the risk-taker in me beckons. *This could be the only time he shows up in daylight. Stretch yourself. Take the shot.* But the more logical part of me disagrees. *No. Don't do it. It's not worth it.*

Wojo reads my mind. "Don't do it, Eva. He's too far. Look, he showed up tonight right before last light, so chances are, he'll be back. We'll get another chance at him tomorrow." It takes everything in me not to attempt the shot.

It was a good call, though. I'd run the risk of making a bad shot if the buck jumped string. What does jumping string mean? Sound travels at around 1,100 feet per second. No matter how quiet a bow's string, a deer is capable of hearing the sound of an arrow being released. If he hears that twang reverberate, in less than a second, he will crouch low, spring off, and make a mad dash for safety. In other words, he'll have jumped string. And by the time the arrow reaches its intended target on his body, the deer is in a different position. The shot might altogether miss him or make a devastating though not fatal injury. Shooting from twenty-five yards versus forty yards away can mean the difference between the deer moving a tiny bit and not interfering with the shot and moving just enough to make the shot ineffective.

Day nine. A light layer of snow covers the ground. The air is bitingly cold. Definitely time to bring out the Heater Body Suit. This drastic change in weather is a good sign, but the morning sit proves uneventful. Disappointing for sure, but I'm not ready to quit. Since I saw the buck yesterday in daylight by this blind, my fingers are crossed.

Around 3:30, well before prime deer activity, Wojo pokes me in the shoulder. "Eve, he's coming in. It's your buck!" My eyes widen as I calm my quickened breath. I carefully slide the bow off my lap, wrapping my fingers tightly around the familiar grip.

Peering through the opening, I see the buck come in with my own eyes. Much of his giant rack of antlers is camouflaged by the barren alpine trees, wet with slushy rain that has just started to fall. He walks toward us, crunching over twigs, weaving his way through the scrawny timber. Heartbeat thumping loudly in my ears, I slowly nock an arrow. I'm ready.

I hear nothing but the patter of raindrops purged from the slate sky. Finally, out from the timberline, the monster buck wanders even closer. He stands in a small opening in the trees about twenty-five yards away, too far to the left of our blind for me to get a shot. I stare, watching him cycle between flicking his ears, twitching his tail, and darting his head left and right. He takes a few steps and stops. Then, picking up his pace, he makes his way to the right. Twenty-five yards away.

Muscle memory leads me without my needing to think. Eyes fixed on the buck, I clip my release* onto the bowstring and draw back. He needs to stop moving for me to make a sure shot. But, he doesn't. I have to be patient and wait for him to stand still, broadside. He keeps walking. My arms start to tremble from a combination of nerves and having to keep my bow at full draw. And then, without warning, he seems to sense something. The elusive buck scampers off and disappears into the trees to my right.

My heart sinks. Tears well up as I let down from full draw. I drop the bow back onto my lap with a groan. Looking back and forth between Wojo and the empty field in front of me, I feel like a failure. I watch the rain season the earth, slippery and wet, as the skinny trees blur in my vision. *This is ridiculous. I had him. He was in my sights.*

And then, movement. Blinking my eyes dry, I see the buck reappear to the right of the blind. And, to my delight, he begins to trek toward the other side.

I regain focus as I draw my bow for the second time. My hand grazes my cheek, my shoulders and upper back muscles taut. The buck is still. This time he's only twenty-three yards away. His rack dips low toward the ground, his body in a textbook broadside position. The clock starts ticking. It's time. Looking through the peep sight, I can see the buck's chest heave with every breath. Being this up-close-and-personal evokes a lot more emotions than staring at wild

---

* A release is a trigger-like device attached to the archer's shooting hand that helps draw back the bow and fire arrows.

game a hundred yards away. Sometimes it feels too close for comfort. Trying to focus on a close shot is tricky; many experienced hunters will say this. My hands begin a steady quake—slow but enough to prevent me from taking a good shot. I try to calm down. *It's just a target, Eva. It's just a target.* I finally reach the necessary, euphoric state of calm. I have just enough time to aim a few inches behind the buck's shoulder and release the arrow with a slow and steady squeeze.

The shot feels good. The arrow spins a lethal and accurate route in flight, the faint *twang* ringing in my ears. In a split second, I notice that the buck is gone. My stomach flips. He jumped string.

Vision blurred from the rush of adrenaline beginning its descent, I don't know where he went. "Did I get him?" I ask Wojo, my breath uneven. I feel light-headed, and the darkness of the ground blind begins to close in on me.

"I think so," he replies, excited.

I'm not so sure.

When you're bow hunting, it's always best to wait awhile after the shot before approaching the animal. If you look for it too quickly, the animal might experience a rush of adrenaline and keep moving, even if you made a great shot. This rarely happens when using a gun. A perfectly placed shot with a firearm will usually make a big enough impact for the animal to go down immediately. So we wait. Thirty minutes pass. An eternity. A dusting of snow begins to blanket the ground.

Finally, we emerge from the dark blind, following the drops of blood from where the shot took place. Connecting the dots from one spot to the next, I wince as the wind nips my face.

As I walk through the maze of trees, I see a grand spread of antlers. I point to the downed buck. "Wojo, look at him!" Even though he jumped string and my arrow hit a few inches higher than where I had aimed, I still made a double-lung shot. This was the biggest buck I had harvested at the time of this writing, based on the Boone and Crockett system, scoring 162 2/8 to be exact.

I bend low, brushing my fingers over the buck's antlers. His hair covered with snow, his body still warm, he's a beauty. His face is weathered and scarred from past fights. I stroke the deer's fur, thinking of my dad and Tim, who both would have loved to be there in that moment.

The hunt ends exactly how I had prayed it would. One beautiful old buck. I thank God for creating this animal and the animal for giving its life to help feed our family for a long time to come. As with harvesting crops, you're unlikely to experience a closer connection to your food than a moment like this. How better to appreciate what you put into your body than by closing the gap between the meat you eat and the animal it came from? I'm proud to be a hunter.

After the handful of whitetail hunts I've posted about on social media, some unkind comments arose along the lines that I "hunt bucks tied up to a fence in the zoo," wildly minimizing my achievement. In fact, after this particular trip, some anti-hunters commented:

"You killed an unsuspecting, defenseless creature. You're a real tough, cool cookie, and by that I mean loser."

"How much did u have to pay to shoot that?"

"How can people be happy to kill innocent life! I'll never understand that!"

People who make comments like these lack perspective. They aren't there when I sit in the cold and the dark day after day waiting for one mature deer to show up. They aren't there when I spend countless hours shooting my bow so I can make one clean shot. They aren't there when I wrestle with making the right decision about how far away I can accurately shoot or letting a nice buck walk away because it's too young.

I've learned over the years that people can always find a reason to speak up against something they don't agree with. Especially if it's something a person believes with deep conviction. But no matter how well prepared I am for the criticism, I still get shocked by how low some people will go.

HATERS HATE

You have enemies? Good. That means you've
stood up for something, sometime in your life.[1]

—WINSTON CHURCHILL

EASTERN NORTH CAROLINA, 2014

*"You are going to come across a lot of people who won't like you.
Critics are going to pop up left and right. They're going to say terrible
things. Trust me."*

It was only five years earlier that I'd sat in Dad's taxidermy-
cluttered office and he'd warned me about the resistance that
would follow my decision to hunt. I had listened to every
word he said. But I just didn't really get it.

When I started posting on social media around 2009, my
Facebook account was private. I had a small following, and
I rarely received negative comments about hunting or anything else. But the following year, when I created my public Facebook page, suddenly anyone could join and throw
in their two cents. To be fair, I knew a public page was just
that, public, and that I'd start getting comments from haters
preaching the evils of hunting. But as much as I'd accepted

that inevitability in theory, I wasn't prepared for what would actually come.

My posts were pretty tame. Still are. Coupled with a mouth-watering photo of venison enchiladas, I'd write, "Look what's for dinner! I hunt it. I cook it. I eat it. I love it!" Sometimes I'd feature a fellow hunter and his or her adventures. And, of course, I'd always post photos from my own adventures hunting around the world, including any animals I had harvested.

Over time, the number of my followers grew. People from all corners of the world joined my page and shared their passion for hunting and the great outdoors.

It's awesome you hunt with your dad! I hope my daughter hunts with me someday.

Welcome to the world of hunters! You'll never look back!

Keep up the good hunting! We need more women hunters!

But other folks—including attention-hungry Internet trolls, anti-hunters who rally behind certain organizations, and random strangers—started hurling hate in my direction. At first, the comments were few and far between. Things along the lines of:

How can you murder an animal?

Why kill an innocent animal when you can get meat from the grocery store?

Fellow hunters would immediately respond in my defense. It was like being surrounded by an army of loyal friends. And I felt just as loyal in return. At the same time, the more people who liked my page and reached out in support, the greater the number of haters who did the opposite. It seemed an exponential progression of hostility.

Around the end of 2010, things got more heated when anti-hunters started posting pictures of me on their websites and social-media pages. All of a sudden, the comments became a lot more personal.

Eva is a murderer!

What c**t would kill these helpless animals?

You are a horrible, horrible person!

Anti-hunting hatred would leak onto my Facebook page and my friends and supporters would stick up for me and fend off the negativity. In a few days, it would be old news. The anti-hunters would leave me alone for a while. But a few weeks later, the same thing would happen again. Eventually, I got used to the cycle, which continues to this day.

I've never made a big issue of this because it seemed like a waste of time. Instead of addressing the negative comments, I'd highlight the girls who weren't embarrassed anymore to tell others they liked to hunt or the women who told me they'd started hunting to provide their family with organic wild game. I kept my page G-rated, informative, and, I hoped, entertaining to hunters young and old.

Growing up, I'd faced my share of criticism. Born with a naturally muscular physique, I've never been skinny. I never focused on my body shape, so it was never an issue. Over the years, however, certain people started making negative comments about my appearance. A friend's brother called me a "fat f**k" when I was eight. In high school some boys made fun of my "manly" legs. For the most part, I've always had a healthy self-esteem, but I'll admit, these words hurt. While getting made fun of in my teen years was somewhat expected, I was sucker punched by more criticism when I was twenty. After lifting me in a routine during dance practice, the male dancer I was coupled with said in a loud voice, "Eva, you feel heavy. What have you been eating?" I was humiliated. I barely had time to digest his comment when he grabbed my stomach through my leotard. Pinching nothing more than skin, he said, "Seriously, Eva. What's this? You've obviously been eating junk food." I blushed while a few other dancers nearby snickered. The comments about my body never stopped. But today, instead of telling me face-to-face, critics shower my social-media pages with their insults. If I'm wearing gym clothes, they say I'm too muscular. If I'm wearing something fitted, I'm too skinny. If I'm wearing hunting clothes, they say I've put on weight. Fit-shaming, fat-shaming, skinny-shaming—I've heard it all.

Criticism can arise in many different forms at any point in your life. People might make fun of your style, tell you you're not good enough, call you dumb, or say you're a nerd. As hurtful as negative words can be, they only mean something if you believe them. It's not easy to hear or read mean or hurtful words—and you can't stop them from coming. But you do have a choice. You can give negative comments power, which will cost you time and energy that you can never get back, or you can allow them to push you forward and continue to follow your own path. The choice is yours.

While the 2014 white-tailed-deer hunt I talked about in Chapter 7 garnered its fair share of negative comments, the backlash increased to a shocking degree after a bear hunt a few weeks later. Here's how it all began.

One day, I received an e-mail from a North Carolina farmer asking for help. The area where he lived was overrun with black bears, causing over a million dollars in damage from ruined crops. If such bears are not harvested and utilized by hunters, local farmers have only one option: get a permit to shoot the animals in the field out of season and leave them there. And with that, the bear meat is wasted, zero jobs are produced, and zero revenue is generated for the county.

As more wildland is developed and roadways built, it's critical to manage the North American bear population to avoid crop damage and protect humans from bear-related motor-vehicle collisions and infiltration into residential areas. Biologists at the North Carolina Wildlife Resources Commission have a complex system in place to collect data on bears. Coupled with their research, they rely on an interesting source to provide about 90 percent of additional information: hunters.[2] Hunters are required to bring the bears they harvest to a local check station to get the animal weighed and premolars taken out. This procedure determines the animal's age and other empirical data that help biologists make science-based decisions on how to help manage the bear population.

In November 2014, I went on a spot-and-stalk hunt on the North Carolina farmer's property and harvested my biggest bear, 510 pounds to be exact. As did all my other hunts, this experience raised funds for wildlife-management programs by my purchasing of a hunting license, bear tag, and ammunition, in addition to assisting with the overpopulation of bears in the area and providing the local community with the meat.

Just as I'd done on previous hunts, I took a picture with the bear and typed the caption, *There's no way to fake this photo . . . he is JUST as big as he looks!* Not long after I posted that on social media, my phone was flooded with a barrage of *dings* announcing incoming texts and voice mails. Eager to find what I expected to be exciting news, I tapped a finger on the first message. A friend told me to check my Facebook account. After logging on, I noticed an outpouring of comments in response to my latest post. When I read the first, I almost dropped my phone. *Did this person talk to his mother with that mouth?* I paused for a second, wondering if I'd written something offensive without realizing it. My eyes fell on the next comment. More shock. *How could someone say that about someone they'd never met?* Why was this bear hunt causing so much hatred?

The photo was going viral and being shared on a number of anti-hunting websites. My entire Facebook wall was full of ugly, mean remarks. I received thousands of death threats. Some anti-hunters hoped I'd be raped. Others suggested that my mom should die for having given birth to me. I could fill a chapter with their awful comments, but here are a few:

This is disgraceful. Let's hope someone hunts her so then they have a trophy.

I'd love to see the picture in reverse, her slumped lifeless . . .

That bear didn't deserve that.

You are an idiot.

How would you like to be gunned down while minding your own business?

No wonder you hunt . . . you have a horse face and look like a transsexual.

You're a psychopath, and you deserve a long and painful death.

F**k you, ditzy c**t. If I had a rifle I'd shoot you right in your ugly face. Please, just die.

I hope you get cancer in your p***y and your kids end up being retarded.

Though I'd received a slew of anti-hunting remarks over the years, for some reason this bear hunt garnered the most negative attention. Might have something to do with the fact that many people humanize these animals, associating them with Winnie the Pooh or a plump and cuddly stuffed animal. But bears are not so harmless. You can't snuggle up to them at night. You can't drag them around with you as a security prop. And, contrary to a popular TV commercial, they certainly don't use toilet paper to take care of business in the woods. Bears are aggressive animals. Not only will they kill cubs to get what they want, they've also killed a number of human beings. I assumed the outrage would quiet down over the next few days, but it didn't. More people posted comments, each more sick and twisted than the last.

I was torn. On one hand, I didn't want to respond to negativity. I knew the deal. Anything I said or wrote in self-defense would just fuel more vicious hate. On the other hand, I didn't want to ignore the situation.

Dad offered advice. "You know the background story about those bears, Eve. You know what you did was a good thing. Don't let the anti-hunters get inside your head. That's what they want. Let it roll off your back."

I understood his point, but I felt I needed to do more. After much thought, I posted a picture of me and my shih tzu puppy and typed:

An anti-hunter just told me to, and I quote, "kill that worthless little dog you have" instead of the bear I just hunted in NC. Apparently, hunting a bear, eating/donating all of the meat, and putting money toward conservation is a bad thing, but killing my puppy is okay. If this logic isn't totally insane, I don't know what is.

The post attracted 33.6 thousand likes and 4.6 thousand comments, most of them positive. A media whirlwind erupted. *TheBlaze* picked up the story. Then I was invited for an interview on *Fox & Friends,* my first major, mainstream television appearance. I never expected to be given the opportunity to share my passion for hunting on such a grand stage. Being grateful for the experience helped quell my nerves.

"What do you have to say to people who share anti-hunting sentiments?" one of the hosts asked.

"If anything, it makes me sad. The people who are saying these things are showing hatred because they don't understand why we hunt. They don't understand the good things we're doing, like feeding our families and conservation. So instead of asking questions and trying to learn about it, they say mean and aggressive things. I don't think they would say those things if they were familiar with the meaning of hunting."

"What's the lesson to you for responding to this kind of abusive behavior?"

"The biggest thing is, what we're doing is a good thing. We raise tons of money for conservation every year, so when anti-hunters are fighting us, they're technically fighting our contribution to wildlife."

The interview aired on multiple national networks and online news channels from ABC's *Nightline* to GrindTV. The support I received in response was staggering. Oh, sure, I still received negative comments and more death threats, but the encouragement that followed transcended the scorn.

All that media attention sparked a movement within the hunting industry. I was so inspired, I added a new product to our merchandise, a T-shirt boasting the comment I'LL NEVER APOLOGIZE FOR BEING A HUNTER. Sales skyrocketed. It's our biggest-selling product to date. I was proud to donate a portion of the proceeds to Freedom Hunters, a charitable organization that honors both active-duty soldiers and combat veterans and their families. The way I see it, these venomous anti-hunters created a marketing campaign for me—for free, no less—that motivated hunters to band together and support what they do. While haters may have hoped their words would scare me away, instead they inspired me to promote the lifestyle even more—and help a few veterans and their families in the process.

Steve Jobs said, "Don't let the noise of others' opinions drown out your own inner voice . . . have the courage to follow your heart and intuition."[3] When the destructive verbal storm erupted, I was faced with a decision. I could have shut down my Facebook page. I could have retreated. I could have kept silent. Instead, I made the choice to take a stand. It wasn't easy. I didn't know how it would end. I never expected millions of hunters to join me and put their own necks on the line to support our community. And I definitely never expected a change of heart from those who were on the fence about hunting. But during this time, one of my childhood friends, a devout vegan with absolutely no interest in hunting, e-mailed me. She told me that after watching the interview about the bear hunt, she began to understand why hunters were critical to conservation and why hunting was important.

Look, anti-hunting extremists aren't bad people. If anything, I believe many of them are naïve and uneducated. They don't know the facts behind ethical hunting. A human being's primitive instinct is to fear the unknown. This is what drives extremists of all sorts—and often from behind a computer screen, which takes a lot less courage than saying these things to someone face-to-face. Fortunately, for me and many fellow-hunters, this tactic doesn't work. If someone doesn't want to hunt, that's fine. If someone doesn't think hunting is right, though I personally disagree, I still believe we can coexist without hurling insults at one another.

> > >

When I was in Russia, I found it hard to explain what I did for a living. Hunting in that part of the world is a predominantly male pastime. (Ironically, though, I just learned that what is thought to be the first Russian women's hunting club was formed in 2014 only 250 miles away from where I lived in Magnitogorsk.[4] Go, female hunters!) When I told Tim's Russian teammates and their wives that I had a career in the outdoor/hunting industry, they would respond with strange looks. For the longest time, instead of greeting me with a simple hello, one hockey player would shape his fingers in the form of a gun, and say "Bang! Bang! Bang! Big hunter girl!" Then he'd walk away, laughing.

I had better luck explaining why I hunt when Tim accepted an offer to play for the Philadelphia Flyers and we moved back to North America in 2015. One weekend, when Tim and a bunch of his teammates were out of town, I invited the players' wives and girlfriends over to my house for a girls-only night to celebrate the holidays. This was the first Christmas in two years that I wasn't overseas, with limited decoration options, so I may or may not have gone a little bonkers tossing up lights here and tinsel there, blitzing our Christmas tree with every ornament under the sun. Next to the cheese platters, plates of crudités, and chips and dips, I placed my (if I may be so bold as to say) world-famous elk chili, from an elk I'd hunted in Utah, and venison summer sausage from a deer I'd harvested in Texas.

Then, during the small talk with the ten or so ladies holding wineglasses and relaxing on couches, I learned that one of my guests was a pescatarian, whose diet includes fish but no other meat. Feeling bad that she was stuck with a limited menu, I found her in the kitchen. As this young woman reached for a cube of cheddar, I tapped her arm. "I am so sorry. I had no idea you only eat fish."

"It's okay," she replied, gracious and sweet. "There's plenty of cheese and veggies that I can eat."

"So, how long have you been a pescatarian?"

"About ten years."

"I'm curious. Why don't you eat meat?" I wasn't trying

to sway her into the meat-eating club. I genuinely wanted to know. Over the years I've met a number of people who have sworn off meat for different reasons, whether thinking meat is unhealthy or the practice of killing animals is inhumane. If you remember, my mom was a vegetarian before she met Dad. She didn't eat meat because she wanted to save animals from being bred and slaughtered for consumption. Though her reasons were legitimate, the lack of protein in her diet made her sick all the time. Once she learned the fundamentals of responsible hunting and started eating wild game, she felt much better. I enjoy learning about people's "whys" and was curious to hear what this young woman had to say.

"When I was in high school," she began, "I watched a documentary about how certain animals were raised in horrible conditions and slaughtered mercilessly. Honestly, it was heartbreaking and disgusting. That day I vowed I'd never eat meat again. I never have."

I told her that I'd seen that type of documentary myself. They're very hard to watch. "One of the reasons I hunt is because I eat organic. And I like to know where my meat comes from."

As I told her about the benefits of eating wild game I harvest myself, the rest of the women began to gather around the island in the kitchen. They munched on the elk and venison apps, ears tuned in to the conversation.

"You know," the pescatarian began, "I respect your choice. It makes sense. And it's probably a lot easier for you to get your protein in, too!" Then she did something that blew my mind. After ten years of not touching meat, she smiled wide and said, "Okay, let me try some of that chili."

I couldn't have been more delighted. I scooped a small spoonful of elk chili on top of a bigger scoop of brown rice and handed her the bowl.

Before she put the spoon to her mouth, I blurted out, "Seriously, you don't have to finish it if you don't want to. And if you don't like it, I won't get offended. I promise!"

"Okay," she said with a chuckle. And on center stage, with ten women watching, she slowly chewed a mouthful of my elk chili.

Would she like it? Would she hate it? Would she regret breaking her commitment?

After swallowing, she said, "Wow! This is amazing!" Then she dug into her bowl and took another bite. Then another. Finally—music to my ears—she said the words I love hearing most after someone eats a meal I've prepared: "May I have some more?"

I sent this pescatarian-turned-wild-game-eater home that night with a few packages of ground elk so she and her boyfriend could cook it themselves. I can't tell you how much elk and deer I gave away to our friends that year after similar conversations. I was grateful to be able to share the rewards of the lifestyle I'd embraced.

Being bombarded by radical anti-hunting opinions has only strengthened my commitment. I've learned that if you make an intentional decision to live a certain way, people who don't understand it will often make you feel like an outcast. This can cross over to any and every choice you make.

Some people won't like the clothes you wear. Or the faith you profess. Or how you parent. But we have to trust our own instincts. We have to trust that the decisions we make are the right decisions for us. This is how we live on purpose. Instead of choosing to focus on destructive criticism, we can focus on choosing our own destiny. On forging our own path. On pioneering the ways in which we intend to live our lives.

Sadly, I've also learned that barbs can come from almost anywhere. Being criticized by an anti-hunter is one thing. Being the target of friendly fire can wound on a deeper level. Hunters who attack other hunters commit a disservice to the hunting community. Every hunter has his or her own approach to the lifestyle. As long as we honor one another and the rules of our craft, it doesn't matter whether we're old or young, male or female, use different brands of gear, hold a gun or a bow, hunt three thousand miles from home or in our own backyard. We are all hunters. There is no need to shame someone who may do things a little differently.

I've read comments from men who suggested I'm not a real hunter and that I'm only doing it for attention. I've heard people discuss other women hunters in the field, deciding which of them are authentic and which are not. The fact that sometimes these comments include me doesn't affect my life much, but what bothers me is the idea that anyone thinks that he or she can judge who is or is not a hunter. There are so many people out there who regularly attack hunters; we don't need our own team embarrassing or slandering us.

Hunters need to unite. We need to stand up for one

another. We need to show our support for new hunters. We need to celebrate girls and women who want to hunt, who've chosen to go against the grain of middle-age-male stereotypes and follow their passion.

> > >

For a long time, the hunting industry was gridlocked when it came to recognizing female hunters. It's only been in the last few years that great strides have been made to provide girls and women with gear and clothing that excel in both performance and fit. I can remember well the challenge I faced even as a little girl in getting outfitted for our family hunting trips.

When I was ten, I remember groaning, "It's still too big!" to my mother while pulling on a smaller size of my brother's camo hunting pants. Surrounded by four circular clothing racks in the boys' section of an outdoor store, Mom sighed. "Okay," she said, rummaging through the camouflage clothing. "How about these?" She held up a pair of extra-small pants.

I poked a foot through one opening, then the other. Hoisting the waist up with my tiny hands, I shook my head. "See? Still too big."

"Well, it's either these or nothing. They don't have anything for girls." Back then, the girl's section carried only pink and purple tees and hoodies, fuzzy hats, and warm gloves.

Years later, I noticed a bigger selection of hunting clothing available for women, but the designers still didn't get it right. The great-fitting pants I wore trekking over hills in Africa weren't stretchy or breathable enough for the movement required. And the jacket that looked and felt great in a mild climate absent of precipitation didn't protect me from the biting cold in the woods of Saskatchewan or the torrential downpours in the Yukon (an adventure to come in the next chapter). But with more and more female hunters showing up in the field, change was imminent.

In 2001, there were only 1.8 million registered female hunters in the United States. In 2013, the number almost doubled to 3.3 million.[5] The National Sporting Goods Association reported that the sales of women's hunting apparel and gear grew more than 43 percent between 2003 and 2013. Today women are the fastest-growing demographic in the hunting industry.[6]

Statistics aside, I've witnessed this spike firsthand. Over the last few years, I've met more and more girls and women at hunting and outdoor trade shows. These weren't wives accompanying their husbands as a favor, or daughters who were dragged there against their will. These were females pursuing the lifestyle for themselves. And the products are starting to respond accordingly.

Until the past few years, the common design approach toward this demographic was simple: shrink it and pink it. It's a bad strategy. Buying a smaller version of a man's bow, firearm, or hunting jacket that's splashed with magenta, cottoncandy pink, or blush doesn't necessarily equal a great product that will perform up to par, nor is it likely to configure to a woman's specific needs.

I noticed a change in products around 2012. Taking note of and filling the niche in the hunting market, Under Armour, for example, started selling clothes made to fit the body shape of a woman, taking into account her curves yet focusing on performance. Companies like Cabela's began to sell gear meant specifically for women, such as guns that were lighter and smaller but just as effective as men's gear. This was great stuff.

The problem I had was finding a compound bow that suited my style of hunting.

For years, as hard as I looked, I couldn't find a premium compound bow that was made for a woman yet matched the performance of a men's model. Please know that I am not against budget hunting gear, nor do I believe that a high price tag always guarantees the best quality in design or mechanics. But for hunting large game animals, efficiency and accuracy are paramount. I'm all about making a great shot on the first try. And I've found that the higher-end bows with the latest and greatest inventions offer the best, most consistent performance. I need a bow with a smooth draw. It must be quiet and lightweight. It must minimize torque and offer a remarkably fast arrow speed. I could talk about the different tech specs of a bow's performance all day long, but then this book would never end.

Up until a few years ago, the best bow marketed for women was markedly slower and offered much less, performance-wise, than the men's model. It also retailed for around $600, while the men's sold for $1,000 and higher. It felt as if the industry didn't see women as good enough hunters to require a high-quality product. I was disappointed in this. And I wasn't the only one.

Around this time, Bowtech, a leading bow manufacturer, noticed that more and more women were not only hunting, but taking up archery. In 2012, 18.9 million people in the United States (or 8 percent of the population) shot archery or bow hunted. Thanks in part to Katniss Everdeen and the popular *The Hunger Games* franchise, by 2014, that total jumped to 21.6 million (78 percent male, 22 percent female). According to the Archery Trade Association, four million women are currently involved in archery either as a target sport or as bow hunters. Appreciating the growth in women's archery and recognizing the untapped market for high-end bows for these customers, Bowtech took action.

On January 8, 2015, two months after the backlash from my bear hunt, I was scheduled to launch a new product at the Archery Trade Association (ATA) expo. Doors opened to the Indiana Convention Center at 8:30 a.m. I arrived earlier, welcoming the warm air gusting through the venue, considering the subzero temperature outside. The space burgeoned with vendors, reps, and booths. Setup was almost complete as men and women rushed around to make final preparations. Schedules were triple-checked. Merchandise was repositioned. Presentations and sound checks were finalized.

"Eva! Eva!" Jeff Suiter, the director of marketing at Bowtech, jogged toward me. For the last year, he and I had been in talks with reps and engineers from the company to help design a high-end compound bow for women. For months, we exchanged ideas and made tweaks. Finally, we submitted our blueprint to the engineers. This day in January 2015 would be our first chance to see the creation we had toiled over for a year.

Jeff was accompanied by the chief engineer responsible for physically making the bow. After exchanging pleasantries, we got down to bow talk. "This has been such a long time coming, Eva," Jeff said, clapping his hands together in anticipation. "We really think you're going to love this bow. Ready to check it out?"

"I can't believe I finally get to hold it in my own hands! This is insane!"

We walked into a five-by-seven room at the far end of the booth designated for Bowtech employees. On a long table bordered by eight chairs lay a bow. *The* bow. My hands shook as I walked toward this incredible piece of equipment. I don't know if Jeff was saying anything, but I was tongue-tied. And that's not something that happens often. Even from a few feet away, the bow looked glorious, a picture-perfect, no-nonsense hunting machine. The rest of the surroundings seemed to dim as an imaginary spotlight of ethereal proportions homed in on the modern-day version of stick and string.

Okay, bear with me while I nerd out for a moment, because the bow we created deserves to be bragged about.

The electric-blue cams* and other accents stood out on the sleek black finish. Even without accessorizing gadgets and

---

* In a compound bow, cams are perfectly symmetrical wheels on the ends of a bow that are designed to create a "let off" at the end of the draw, making it easier to hold a bow at a certain weight for a longer period of time.

gizmos such as a stabilizer and sights, the design itself was impressive. I picked up the bow, which comes in draw weights of forty, fifty, and sixty pounds. I couldn't believe how lightweight it was. With a shooting speed of 332 feet per second, this bow was a speed demon. Aside from weighing less and having a shorter draw length than a high-end men's model, this bow was every bit as fast and well-designed.

I turned the bow over and over in my hands, my eyes glued to the EVA SHOCKEY SIGNATURE SERIES (ESSS) stamped across the top. The butterflies in my stomach collided with one another. I wanted to put this baby to work.

Jeff read my mind. "Do you want to shoot it?"

"Absolutely!"

Jeff led me to the archery lanes about twenty yards away. Throughout the day they would be packed with expo attendees testing out different bows at a ten-yard distance. In this moment, however, the space was empty except for me, Jeff, and a handful of reps from the company. Jeff, a grin plastered on his face, picked up another ESSS bow that was waiting for me, this one outfitted with a sight, a rest, and a stabilizer. Ready for action. "She's all yours."

A hush enveloped the shooting area when I got into position, not a word or a whisper spoken. It was my first time shooting a bow in full makeup and wearing dressy clothes that felt restrictive. But, oh, well. With a deep breath, I drew back, ready to take my first shot at the foam target painted with a bullseye. With a slow squeeze, the arrow released at warp speed, the familiar twang barely audible.

And the arrow hit the mark.

"Oh, my gosh!" I blurted out. "It feels like butter." Smooth as velvet and with an accuracy I had never experienced. It was love at first shot. It's one thing to talk about what you want to see in a high-end bow. It's another thing to hold that bow and draw back, to feel the speed, power, and efficiency for yourself.

Twenty minutes later, on a stage surrounded by about seven hundred manufacturers, retailers, distributors, sales representatives, media folks, and other members of the hunting industry, I was proud to unveil the bow. "This is a huge deal for me to be up here and have the honor of announcing what I'm about to tell you," I said. "This is the first ever signature series bow from Bowtech. It's very close to my heart, because I've been working with them in the design process. This bow is as high end as it gets for the serious female hunter. My prayers have been answered!"

I watched as the audience held out their phones and cameras to snap pictures of the bow. I had attended ATA trade shows over the years with my family, watching others mount platforms to introduce new gear and products. Now I was humbled to be in that same position.

But, I'll say it again. It's not *my* bow. Of course it isn't! It belongs to serious women hunters everywhere. And in a climate where too many people are still inclined to shame us or reach out in hate, that moment was a reminder to me of why we hunt, why we matter, and why we wouldn't trade this life for all the approval in the world.

9

A MOOSE AT MY WEDDING

The mountains are calling and I must go.

—JOHN MUIR

YUKON TERRITORY, CANADA, SEPTEMBER 2014
⟩⟩

Say good-bye to civilization, I tell myself on the dock, and then I duck into the single-engine floatplane moored there.

I prop my legs on top of a canvas duffle bag, which is stacked on top of a bin full of ammo that's sandwiched between a propane tank and a rifle case. Every inch of space is occupied by humans or gear. Two cameramen squeeze in behind me. Dad sits alongside the pilot.

Once aloft, I press my nose against a Plexiglas window and take in the scenery below. The small town of Mayo in central Yukon, a sparsely populated territory in northwestern Canada, begins to disappear as we climb. Our adventure, in which the comforts of modern times will cease to exist, begins. We fly east, entering the twelve thousand square miles of our family's hunting territory nestled in the wild. Because we own the guiding rights to this area in the Yukon, each year we get a certain number of tags to hunt moose, caribou, and grizzly bears. Not only do Dad and I hunt here with a certified guide, which is required in this territory, but fellow hunters can do the same using guides hired by our company. With about seventeen camps throughout the territory offering varying degrees of rusticity, there are plenty of adventures to be made.

This is my fourth season hunting the heavyweight of the North American animal kingdom, the Alaskan-Yukon moose. A bull (male) moose can weigh more than 1,500 pounds, more than the weight of three baby grand pianos. Try skinning and dressing that size beast in the wilderness before grizzlies and wolverines start sniffing around.

The seaplane charts a course over a river flanked by an amphitheater of mountains. Peaks are dusted with snow. Slopes showcase bold shades of autumn. The towering giants dip into deep valleys. No houses, no roadways—nothing but land and water everywhere you look. Animals here roam free. Caribou wander in herds on the alpine tundra. Moose meander through vegetation in the valleys, the bulls usually in bachelor groups unless they're rutting. Then they travel solo, looking for females to pair up with, anywhere from one to twelve. Plodding over the landscape like giants, grizzly bears strip bushes of their berries and tear into carcasses of caribou. Wolves, too, skulk in the shadows, looking for prey.

The plane slides onto the surface of a placid lake and approaches a dock. It's early afternoon. The minute the door opens and we pile out, the bucket brigade begins. The boxes and bags that are crammed into the plane are forked over by one pair of arms to another until, a few minutes later, the plane is empty.

I notice a familiar face by the edge of the dock. "Shane!" I exclaim, dropping a duffle bag to make room for a hug. "How are you?" He'll be my guide this trip.

In welcome, the scruffy-faced man tugs at his baseball cap, its edges frayed and logo unrecognizable from wear. His salt-and-pepper beard and the dirt caked under his fingernails tell me that Shane's been in the bush for a couple of months.

"Doin' great, Eva!" he says warmly while resisting my outstretched arms. "Don't get too close now. Haven't showered in a while."

I laugh, offering a knowing grin. "So, what's the verdict?" I ask. "Has the rut started? Have you called any bulls in?"

"Nah. It's just heating up. They're getting curious, though. It's going to get real good out there in the next few days."

It's September 2014. No one can predict exactly when the rut will begin. Moose up here start rubbing off their velvet as early as the last week in August and as late as the first week of September. The rut breaks out after that. Tasked by nature with amassing a harem of cows to breed with, bulls get loud and aggressive, often sparring with competing bulls. Typically, one or more smaller bulls will hang around these groups, hoping to steal a cow if they get a chance. During the rut, it's pretty easy to lure a bull closer by calling him. Either you vocalize a bull's low-pitched grunt, beat the brush with a canoe paddle, or mimic the sound of a cow's low moan. Curious, the bull will investigate the source of the sound to see whether it's a competitor to chase off or a cow with girlfriend potential.

Once the plane has been reloaded with leftovers from the previous hunt, the aircraft roars across the lake and up over the mountains standing guard over this wilderness kingdom. By then, the silence has returned. We are alone in the middle of nowhere. For me, panic sets in. It's fleeting, but it happens every time.

Remembering to breathe, I inhale sharply. I know what's coming. Packing and repacking multiple times for multiple camps up in these mountains. Sleeping atop a mattress of earth. Sharp winds that seem to cut skin and drown out conversation. Days of endless dirt and grime. Hours and hours of strenuous hikes, muscles burning. Meals eaten straight out of unlabeled cans. And, if we get lucky, the sweat and toil of skinning and dressing a bull moose in the middle of nowhere.

When you're this far from civilization, there's no one waiting to help if something goes wrong. Getting a clear signal on the satellite phone often takes thirty minutes, and even with the phone, you're on your own. You can't call an ambulance, and a rescue will take days. What you're left with is a first-aid kit and whatever survival skills you have. Which is why the moment that floatplane lifts off, and I feel that stab of panic, I always remind myself of our company's five rules: *Safety. Safety. Safety. Safety. Safety.*

Yukon regulations forbid hunting sooner than six hours after arriving at camp in an aircraft (to prevent hunters from spotting targets by plane), so the rest of the day involves prep and logistics. Shane arranges sleeping accommodations. "We left the far cabin for you, Eva. Since you're the closest to the bush, keep a gun around just in case a grizzly decides to visit." The threat from these mammoth creatures is real. Last year, one started poking around a camp in the middle of the night. The guide was startled awake by the sound of his cabin door being ripped from its bolts and had no choice but to shoot the grizzly as it charged.

"Jim, we left you your usual bunk in the cook shack. We know the drill."

"But that's the only cabin with a heater," I complain half-jokingly.

Dad laughs. "Seniority rules."

This particular camp consists of three cabins, all roughly constructed, sporting impressive racks of moose antlers (found from wolf kills) over the doorways. Fitting decor. Two eight-by-eight cabins, walls covered in plywood sheathing, offer simple wooden bed frames. The third is bigger. A cook shack—which also houses a cot in the back of the room, where Dad sleeps—is stocked from top to bottom with nonperishable food and supplies, two or three guns, and boxes of ammo. Our meals in base camp are relatively elaborate (think cooked eggs and a fresh veggie or two) thanks to a propane stove and space that we don't have when we move out to what we call spike camp, which is our semipermanent secondary campsite in the middle of the bush.

A long table covered with a faded vinyl tablecloth invites us to eat together, share hunting stories, and make plans over steaming mugs of coffee. Water for cooking, drinking, and cleaning comes from the glacier-fed creek above the lake.

You learn quickly to use the same bowl and piece of silverware every time you eat—the fewer you use, the fewer you have to clean. Eating straight from a can works even better.

The meat shed stands forty yards away from the cabins. Quartered animals are hung from the ceiling by an intricate setup of hooks and ropes, away from hungry grizzly bears and other curious scavengers. We've had to replace the door several times thanks to these animals. At the top of the food chain, Yukon grizzlies can get as big as nine feet tall, although more commonly seven or eight. These predatory powerhouses have a bad habit of demolishing anything in their path. In addition to breaking doors, grizzlies have smashed windows and shredded countless tents over the years.

Dumping my fifty-pound duffle bag onto the solid wood bed frame in my cabin, I handpick items needed for spike camp the next day. I pat the inside pocket of the bag to make sure my hunting tags are there—one for a moose, one for a caribou (in case we see one en route to hunt a moose), and one for a bear (in case one gets too close and starts charging). *Check.* Now out come the long johns and rain gear.

I hear footsteps approaching over the parched grass and loose gravel outside. "Getting ready for tomorrow?" Shane asks, popping his head in the doorway.

As much as I love a good adventure, I'm not the biggest fan of sleeping on damp earth with only a thin piece of nylon tent separating me from the grizzlies. We usually travel at least four hours from base camp to look for moose. By the time we find one, which can take days of searching, at least another four hours lie ahead to skin, butcher, and pack up the meat. Nine times out of ten it's dark by then, so we have no choice but to camp beside the kill in the mountains. This is what we call bush pig camp, a bare-bones shelter of just a few pup tents. It feels a lot like sleeping right beside the bait in an enormous predator trap.

As I toss a hairbrush and a stick of deodorant into the can't-take-to-spike-camp pile, I say, as sweet as pie, "How about, instead, we take the Argos (the brand of all-terrain vehicles we use here) down the valley and see if we can get a moose, then come back to base camp tomorrow night and stay in our cabins?"

He laughs. "Good one, Eva."

I try to get some sleep that night, my back stiff against the rigid bed frame. This is the most comfortable I will be for the next week. We've got long days ahead.

> > >

The morning sun rises slowly over the landscape, glimmering into the lake, which is as smooth as glass. Sleepy, I reach for the cup of water I brought with me to bed hours ago. It's frozen solid. I sigh, stretching out my stiff limbs. I smell bacon from two cabins down.

We all gobble breakfast and run through mental checklists. Then, while Shane cleans off the table, I grab the .300 Win Mag (Winchester Magnum) off the gun rack. It's outfitted with a magazine that holds three extra bullets. The scope has been carefully mounted and dialed in so that it shoots two inches high at a hundred yards, dead-on at two hundred.

Popping five rounds of ammo into my pants pocket, I leave the gun's chamber empty and lock on the safety. I finish at the same time that Dad pockets his ammo and slings an extra gun onto his shoulder. It's important to have two firearms in case one malfunctions. When you're in the middle of nowhere, you can never be too careful.

Two Argos are parked next to the cabins. These eight-wheeled amphibious vehicles are at home in harsh terrain, traveling up steep slopes and through rushing water with seemingly little effort. I help finish the loading. Squeezing the Trigger Sticks into an empty space, I make sure I can see the canoe paddle somewhere in the mix of big plastic bins filled with supplies, an army of tarps, and game bags of varying sizes. We use the game bags to pack up moose or caribou meat that's been skinned, butchered, and quartered in the field.

A light breeze rustles through camp, the morning song I miss when I'm not outdoors. As the last aromas of breakfast drift away in the air, I begin to think we just might make it out of base camp close to schedule. The Yukon can be a black hole of time. Everything takes longer. The weather is in charge, imposing frequent delays because of snow, wind, or rain. Spend some time out here, and you're forced to learn patience.

"Everyone have their rain gear and sleeping bags?" Dad asks, double-checking the loaded Argos. And with that, we're off.

We begin the four-hour trek down the valley toward spike camp. I don't hear much with the helmet on, just the rumble of the Argo as it navigates its way over rocky creek beds and craggy hills. An hour and a half later, I notice a lookout point where we often stop to glass. It doesn't take long to see a mass of white enter the view of my binoculars. The thick ring of snowy fur around the caribou's neck is unmistakable through the amber and gray willows, their skinny branches trembling in the wind. The animal stands nearly a mile away. Hardened antlers extend impressively toward the sky. Definitely a male. Caribou is the only deer species in which both females and males have antlers, although females' racks are considerably smaller and less complex.

"Wow," Dad whispers. "His tops are huge."

"This is crazy. We just left camp," I say. Spotting a mature bull this early in the hunt never happens.

We watch the caribou walk down through the willows from the crest of the hill. The closer he gets, the better I can make out his antlers. I gasp. "He's got a double shovel* out the front." Not something you see often.

Slinging my bolt-action rifle onto my shoulder, I quietly start to close the now 1,200-yard gap. The terrain is a mix of moss-covered ground and rocks. When I reach a comfortable distance with a clear view of the bull, I shove the Trigger Sticks into the earth. He's motionless. I aim, breathe deeply, and fire. The bullet goes straight through his heart. A perfect shot.

Up close, the bull's large rack is even more remarkable. The tops pan out in a near-palmate fashion, similar to a moose. Impressive, to say the least. After reveling in the

---

* Antlers on adult male caribou showcase a unique configuration of parts described as beams, palms, and points. This includes brow palms (also called *shovels*) that jut out, one on each side, just over the animal's face. Double shovels are rare.

caribou's magnificence and thinking about the fresh, wild-game dinner we'll be enjoying in a few short hours, I realize something. "Hey, guys. We can drive the Argos right up to him! That never happens!"

"You just made our jobs a whole lot easier," Dad replies. "Let's find a flat spot to skin him, rather than up here on the hillside."

It takes about an hour and a half to skin and quarter the animal. This bull provides us with over two hundred and fifty pounds of packable meat. With enough daylight left, we head back to base camp, where the quartered caribou is hung in the meat shed to cool. Lowering meat temperature to air temperature, somewhere in the forties at this point, is key to preventing spoilage.

"My prayers have been answered!" I boast at dinner, chewing tender meat off a barbecued rib. "Another night in the palace with the best meat on earth!"

"We got lucky," Dad says. Then he points out the window toward the other two rustic cabins. "Enjoy it while it lasts. No guff, after tonight, these luxurious accommodations are over. Tomorrow morning, we leave at eight sharp. Let's get to spike camp early enough to set up and hunt before sunset."

"Sounds good," I say, dipping my spoon into mashed potatoes.

> > >

The next morning is like déjà vu. Driving two hours north of base camp brings us to a lookout point where we can see across to the other side of the valley below. Leaving the Argos, we begin to hike. We're heading toward a narrow ledge we can see that juts off the jagged face of the mountain. The farther we ascend through dense mountain birch and willow, the more my leg muscles burn. At somewhere around 5,500 feet—an ideal elevation for glassing into the valleys below—I turn and look around just before we reach the narrow surface protruding from the crest. A blast of wind almost makes me tumble, but I dig the heels of my boots into the ground and gape at the beauty of the Yukon.

The valley below, flecked with reds and golds and streaked with green, seems miles away. I feel closer to heaven than earth. Breathing deeply, I immerse myself in the stillness. This is a space free of distraction. I finally stop looking at my watch. The Yukon doesn't tell time. It reminds me to slow down and marvel at the masterpiece of God's creation.

The land below is so vast, it seems it would be impossible to spot moose. Anyway, they're usually well camouflaged in tall shrubs or willows. My backpack pressed firmly into the rocky face of the mountain, I sweep my binoculars slowly from left to right. I can see for miles in every direction. But now it's not the majestic mountains that demand my undivided attention, or the azure sky stretched wide and dotted with clouds. I'm looking for a whitish glint, the sun reflecting off smooth beige antlers. This high up, it's likely the most I'll see of a moose.

An hour passes while the three of us wait on the ledge. Nothing. I notice something glimmer in the distance. I blink several times, my eyes still adjusting to glassing through binoculars, and look again. The glimmer is gone. I don't know what it was, if anything, but it wasn't a bull. A sharp blast of wind whips across my face, chafing my already dry skin. While the temperature hovers around a reasonable fifty-something degrees, the wind is a bully. I'm grateful for the multiple layers piled under my heavy camouflage jacket.

Hours of constant scanning and waiting can make your eyes play tricks on you. You can look at the same spot a hundred times and see nothing, but maybe you will on the hundred and first time.

"Anyone see anything?" I ask, wondering if I'm the only one without a moose in my view.

"Nope, nothing over here," Dad says.

"Me, neither," Shane responds.

Finally, we decide to hike back down to the Argos. After carefully making our way down the mountain, we drive on a well-worn and relatively smooth trail that leads eventually to a patch of open space by a small river at the bottom of a valley—the site of a spike camp we've used many times. We are hemmed in by willows. Stretched behind us, a backdrop of peaks powdered with snow. Large rocks, some broken, pepper the ground. We get to work setting up camp.

"Shane," Dad calls out, "you and I will get the tents set up." The two of them plunk down a maze of poles and bulky canvas that will serve as sleeping quarters for Dad and me as well as a makeshift kitchen to cook meals over the propane stove.

I offer to unpack the food barrel, walking toward one of the three fifty-five-gallon steel drums that contain the essentials of spike camp. These barrels are permanent fix-tures. Each is screwed tightly shut to outsmart curious griz-zlies eager to inspect anything unfamiliar.

With a wrench, I muscle the lid off one barrel. I notice that the outside metal is just as dented and scratched up as the year before but not a whole lot worse. Looks like no grizzlies tried to get in this year. Every can in this barrel has been here for at least five years. That means they've frozen and thawed many times. None are labeled; they're so old the labels have worn off—a surprise awaits with every turn of the can opener. I collect an armful of cans and place them by the edge of the partially constructed cook tent. "Can't wait for mystery dinner," I tell the men.

I open another drum and peer into it, disappointed. "Not a ton of kindling left," I mutter. Because it often rains dur-ing hunting season, leaving the wood around camp wet, it's always a good idea to load the vehicles with pieces of dry fire-wood in case we get stuck hours away from spike camp and need to make a fire while setting up bush pig camp.

Shane shrugs. "I guess you'll be lighting fires out there with willow," he says.

After a short glassing session, we return to spike camp for the evening.

"Who's ready for a five-star meal?" Dad asks, stirring a large pot on the small propane camping stove.

Huddled shoulder to shoulder on two cots, our hunt-ing party eagerly awaits Dad's surprise meal. "For you," Dad says, dumping a ladle overflowing with lumpy slop into my metal bowl. I chew slowly, tasting a mix of mushroom soup and green beans. A Vienna sausage or two swim around the stew, adding more texture. This hodgepodge of warmed-up canned foods will also serve as breakfast the next morning. It's gross when you think about it, but—trust me—when you're cold and hungry, it's food fit for a king. Eating canned foods is not high on my list of nutrition priorities, but when I'm stuck in the middle of nowhere, I don't have a choice. Good news is that I remembered the Ziploc bag full of left-over grilled caribou ribs. I pull out my backpack and ration out the pieces to my companions.

We chow down, soon rolling into our sleeping bags to retire for the night. Swaddled in layers of down and wool, warmed by the heat of the potbelly stove, I'm asleep in minutes. If wolves howl nearby or grizzlies slurp from the river twenty yards away, I'll never know it.

That night, I dream of moose.

The morning requires more downsizing. We're heading farther in today. We pack the Argos with two pup tents, tarps, game bags, and a backpack each. Necessities only. I've stuffed my dry bag with an extra pair of pants, a warm jacket, and a couple of unlabeled tin cans of food, taking care to fill up my water bottle from the bubbling river, its banks trimmed this time of year with bright orange soapberries.

As I haul my backpack into the Argo, I notice that the seat cushion is shredded. Four-inch slashes mark the entire right side of the vinyl material.

"Hey," I call out to whoever is closest. "We had a visitor last night!"

"Whoa! I can't believe none of us woke up from the noise!" Shane remarks, setting down the full water jug he just finished carting back from the river. He skims the surface of the ripped material with his fingers. "Look at the size of those claws!"

We agree that it's a good thing we didn't have any fresh meat in camp, or this grizzly would have hung around a lot longer.

"On that note, don't forget to leave your tent doors unzipped," Shane reminds us.

I walk around to each tent, unzipping the door flaps. Don't need any obnoxious grizzlies tearing through the fabric with their six-inch-long claws. Will open doors stop one from shredding the tents? It might. It's a chance we're willing to take.

A cold front has blown in overnight. When we arrived at base camp four days ago, the temperature was in the fifties. Today demands extra layers. Even the warmth of the sun doesn't take the shiver out of the air. Weather in the Yukon abides by no rules. Cloud-free skies one minute can turn into torrential downpours the next. Temperatures can skyrocket or plummet in a few hours. One thing is a near constant—the wind. So no matter what a thermometer reads, it always feels a heck of a lot colder, especially the farther up the mountains we hike.

We roll out of camp at a steady seven-miles-per-hour pace. The next twelve hours are pretty straightforward. We Argo, then hike to different lookout points on a jumble of high peaks, where we glass for a mature bull. By the time the sun slides down behind the mountains in the west, I have seen nothing except some cows and a few young bulls that aren't old enough to shoot.

But the next day, it gets real.

I sit on another lookout point at above five thousand feet. Along with Dad, a few feet away on one side, and Shane on the other, we're scanning the hills. Time passes slowly. Finally, something catches my eye. I blink a few times and take another look. My heart quickens.

"I see a big white spot!" I blurt. "And I'm pretty sure it's moving." Dad and Shane stir to take a look.

"Where are you looking?" Dad asks, pointing his binoculars in the general direction mine face.

"See the big shadowed spot in the middle of the hill face ahead of us? Follow the bottom of that shadow to your five o'clock for about a hundred yards. You'll see a broken stump in a small, open grassy area. Go straight up from there, and he's in the bushes about thirty yards up." I take another sweep of the area and notice more moose. "Looks like he's got a few cows with him."

"Yup," Dad says after a minute or two, "definitely a bull." He whips out the forty-power-magnification spotting scope. "Let's see exactly what we've got," he says, grounding the wide-based, low-clearance tripod in the dirt. One eye closed, dialing the scope of the lens just so, he nods. "Yup. That's definitely a nice bull."

"Let me take a look," I say, scooching toward him, feet and bum moving quickly over the jagged earth. "Holy cow!

Look at those wide, heavy pans.* Long tines, too!" With the largest antlers in the world, an Alaskan-Yukon bull moose's spread can measure over seventy inches. Try to imagine the amount of neck muscle required to hold up seventy-some pounds of antlers.

Trading the spotting scope back for my binoculars, I take stock of the terrain markers near the bull, who is now thrashing his antlers violently against the brush. Moose will do this for a number of reasons, including to mark their territory, to rub velvet off their antlers, or to warn other moose of their presence. A few hundred yards away lies a beaver pond, bordered on one edge with an impressive pile of branches. Two spruce trees are nearby. A hill to the west. As I make mental notes to remember when we make our way down toward the bull, another behemoth enters my line of sight. Not more than a few hundred yards away from the unsuspecting moose, a silver-tipped grizzly bear is munching on berries, pulling up the roots with his claws. We'll have to be on guard as we descend toward the bull.

The crew piles into the two Argos. As we bounce over the choppy landscape, small rocks tumble under the tires. Large ones jut out from the ground like speed bumps. My knuckles are white from their death grip on the side handlebar. Finally, at the end of the craggy slope, we reach level ground and amble up a small hill.

---

* While moose antlers vary in size and shape, most adult males have two main broad pans/palms that have tines, or points, along the outer edge. Smaller palms, or *fronts,* may jut out from under the main palms over the moose's head.

Scouring landscape from a few thousand feet above is different from actually stalking on it. When you get there, the land comes alive. It swallows your previous point of view. The brush is thicker, wider, and terrain markers are not as obvious as they appeared from above.

Dad steps on top of the hood of the Argo to try to spot the moose.

"Two hundred yards to the right of the spruce should be a beaver pond," I say.

"I see the beaver pond but no spruce."

"You've got to be kidding me!"

"There's gotta be another beaver pond nearby," Dad offers. "Let's start backtracking."

We lose time but finally make our way to the last spot we saw the moose. Silence is key. Our boots crunch softly over twigs atop a carpet of moss. We are hyperaware of the grizzly we know is lurking nearby. Every few steps, I squeeze talcum powder into the air. The white dust floats away from me. So far, so good.

I move quietly but quickly. Glancing down at the soft ground, I notice long, narrow grooves in the shape of hooves. Fresh moose tracks. We're close. Another look at the ground startles me. Bigger tracks accompany the moose's, wider and longer than my entire foot. *The grizzly!* I clutch the high-powered rifle tightly in my hands. If he happens to charge, I'm ready. My heart pounds faster and louder with every step.

Eventually we enter a run of tall willows that looms over my head. The grizzly tracks have disappeared, but the moose prints remain. Ears pricked, my eyes dart in every direction.

I weave carefully through the thick brush. Branches slap my face. I feel the slow burn of welts on my cheeks.

Step. Step. Step. The once-piercing blue sky is now muted, the mountains ahead glowing with gold from the sinking sun. There's not much time left.

Suddenly, I can smell the bull. During the rut, bulls mark themselves by scraping out muddy pits and urinating over themselves. Apparently, cows are turned on by this scent. My stomach churning as the noxious scent invades my nostrils, I see something ahead. About a hundred yards away, through the thick brush of willow, huge pans emerge. The spread is magnificent. I count at least ten tines on one antler, some longer than others. This is a big bull. And then, just as quickly as they appear, the antlers disappear into an even taller grove. I can't tell where he went. The wind rushes through the skinny branches as I strain my eyes left and right.

Then I hear something. The distinct sound of antlers being twisted left and right in the thicket resonates in the quiet. This bull suspects an intruder. He wants us to know he's there and that he's in charge of the cows nearby. Beige prongs soar over the tall undergrowth like cupped hands, fingers outstretched. I set up the shooting sticks, the stock of the rifle digging into my shoulder.

The moose is seventy-five yards away. Through the scope, I see him ambling toward us, his antlers rocking slowly back and forth.

Dad holds up the canoe paddle to imitate the white pan of a smaller bull. Suspicious, the bull moves closer. But he stops a few strides away. *Did he catch our scent?* I watch and wait.

My body is calm, but my heart is rushing like a wall of water about to burst a dam. As the bull moves into a slight clearing in the brush, I adjust the sticks and the rifle. I hold the crosshairs steady right behind the bull's shoulder.

"If you've got a shot, take it," Dad says.

I do, but the willows taunt me. *What if a branch gets in the way of the shot?* It's tempting to back off. Instead, I breathe deeply and silence the doubts. My bullet is heavy, and I'm close enough that the scrub won't affect its trajectory.

"I've got the shot," I say, confident. And with a slow squeeze of the trigger, the bullet blasts through the silence. In open space without timberline to muffle the sound, the noise is deafening. The stock kicks back into my shoulder, stunning me for a moment. It's got more power than the .270-caliber I'm used to.

I hear the thud of the bullet as it penetrates the moose. "Holy cow! That was wild!" I burst out, my hands shaking. Drowning out the chatter around me, I take a minute before I approach the bull. My heart races, screaming for deep breaths.

When my adrenaline finally stops pounding, I kneel next to the bull. Shock ripples through my body. He's enormous. He makes a horse look the size of a pony. And his rack? Wider than both my arms outstretched. A coat of tan fur, darkening toward the belly and backside, covers the bull. A moose actually has two layers of fur: on top, a guard layer consisting of hollow hair that's thicker and longer in the winter; underneath, a dense, insulating coat. Even with these layers, the bull's muscular physique is evident to the touch, firm and lean. I grab the sixty-three-inch-long canoe paddle and use it to make a loose measurement of his thirteen-by-twelve-point antlers. "They've got to be at least sixty-three inches wide," I say to the men who have joined me in admiring the majestic beast. The bull's antlers are so heavy, I can't budge them an inch.

This hunt is personal. It's different than the others. While my loved ones and I always eat the meat from every animal I harvest, there's something special about this one. My voice cracks as I announce, "The meat from this moose is going to feed everyone at my wedding next summer!" The men smile as wide as the Yukon.

But the celebration doesn't last long. We all know what's coming. The second you pull the trigger on a moose, the hard work begins.

"Well, we're definitely not getting out of here tonight," Shane comments as a light rain begins to fall.

I look around as daylight fades. We've got to hustle back to the Argos to get the supplies we need for camp. Then four hours of strenuous labor lie ahead. The charcoal sky provides an eerie background as we get to work. We all have tasks, each one as important as the next. In a grassy opening a hundred yards from where the moose lies, I begin to set up bush pig camp.

Guided by headlamps and high beams from the Argos, Shane and Dad slice into the bull's hide with precision. With brawn and grit, they peel back the skin, exposing raw meat marbled with fat.

"Eva," Dad calls out, his fingers curled around a knife

splattered with blood. I quickly abandon tent duty for moose duty.

"Grab this front leg and hold it tight," he says. "If it starts slipping, just let go. Don't grab for it in case you get in the way of the knife."

Wiping away the rain streaming down my forehead, I wrap my hands around the bull's thigh. I'm glad I'm tasked with holding it down. The leg is so heavy, I can barely lift it off the ground.

Dad stretches a thick layer of hide up and out toward Shane. "Hold it high," he says. "I don't want any hair on the meat."

Aware that grizzlies can lurk anywhere, we have to work fast.

As Dad slices away, Shane and I continue to pin down quarters and shift muscle, hide, or bone when needed. The meat is warm, which is nice if your hands are working directly on the moose, as the temperature is falling. Dad finishes detaching a hindquarter, and Shane and I grab it with gloved hands as it dislodges from the body. Carrying what weighs close to a hundred and fifty pounds, we stagger over to the tarp laid out on the ground. Shane grunts as I hold out a breathable four-by-four-foot game bag into which we shove the thick slab of red meat. The most important rule of skinning and gutting a large wild game animal is to keep the meat clean and cool. Ideally, hanging an animal to work on it is best, but there are no trees big or strong enough in this part of the Yukon to support the sheer weight of a moose.

An hour passes as we muscle six or seven hundred pounds

of moose meat into these cloth sacks. The bags are then assembled in a line across the tarp. When the last chunk of meat is packed, I lay another tarp on top to protect the bags from getting wet. But before I do, I can't help but stare in awe at the fifteen-foot row of packed moose.

The pouring rain dyes the soft ground crimson, the smell of blood a magnet for hungry predators. As we finish our work an hour or two past midnight, the wolves are howling. We have no choice but to spend the next few hours guarding our fresh meat.

It's only by a miracle that the willow brush I've collected catches fire. These skeletal branches are barely flammable on their best day, let alone when they're wet. Orange flames lick up over the Yukon earth, dancing toward the midnight sky. I can't feed the flames fast enough. It's the most high-maintenance fire I've ever started, but it's our only option to dry out and cook some dinner.

Before settling into our sleeping bags for a few hours of restless sleep, we sit around the campfire that cooks our dinner. Cuts of moose backstrap are impaled on spare tent pegs around the shooting flames. We haven't eaten in more than twelve hours, but as we settle in to dine on these prime slices of wild game, fresh from the field, we know it's been a good day. We are exhausted but content. As the flames crackle, the moon hovers above, pure white.

In a few days, I'll return to city life, return to my fast-paced schedule and being surrounded by people and needing to remind myself to stop complaining because the line at Starbucks is too long or the traffic is moving too slowly. I will miss the peace and quiet of the wilderness. As the wind rustles through the willow and the masterpiece of the Yukon rests in a soft glow, I am thankful.

No bears or wolves got near our meat that night. And nine months later, eighty-seven loved ones enjoyed the rewards of our hard work. On June 20, 2015, I stood under an oak tree on my childhood property, hand in hand with Tim. Our wedding day. A warm breeze made the lake behind us dance in melodic waves as our closest friends and family members witnessed our exchange of "I do's." For hours we danced to country tunes underneath white lights stretched out through the trees. This Alaskan-Yukon moose took center stage on the buffet table, sliced thin in juicy pieces and accompanied by local salmon and fresh-baked bread from a bakery in town.

It might have been the moose, or it might have been the love, but I still think that was the best meal I've ever tasted.

Hunting does not provide a conventional kind of fun, I'll admit. It's not as relaxing as fanning yourself on a tropical beach with a stream of umbrella-topped drinks that never stops coming. But the rewards are far greater. You're forced to be intensely present. To be in the moment. To take in the fresh air. To celebrate God's creation and the many ways in which it sustains us. Hunting is something that keeps on giving long after the trip is over.

10

DIAMONDS FROM THE SKY

My soul can find no staircase to Heaven
unless it be through Earth's loveliness.

—MICHELANGELO

GILA NATIONAL FOREST, NEW MEXICO, 2016

When I was hiking in South Africa on my first hunting trip, I never would have imagined that, seven years later, I would be climbing mountains in New Mexico—seven months pregnant.

I'll never forget when I first found out I was having a baby. Visions of my cooing and gurgling little one wearing a cute camo onesie danced in my head. I wondered if he or she would be a mini-me or take after my laid-back husband. Celebratory musings aside, I then swept through my hunting calendar in my head. I had an elk hunt in New Mexico scheduled for November. I did the math, realizing I'd be seven months pregnant by then. Would I have to cancel the trip? Would hunting at that point even be physically possible for me?

When I googled what it was like to be seven months pregnant, I almost fell off my chair. *Holy smokes! What did I get myself into?* And how am I supposed to climb a mountain eight thousand feet above sea level with a belly the size of a watermelon? By the third trimester, internal organs—lungs, stomach, and bladder—are squished, squashed, and pushed around to make room for the baby. This internal shifting is physically taxing on the body. Bottom line is that pregnancy is a lot of work, particularly in the third trimester. Drastic changes to the body can make everything you're used to doing a lot harder. Even breathing can become a challenge. My googling session didn't exactly leave me inspired. I wasn't hopeful I could go through with the hunt as planned. So I spent a lot of time thinking about the trip, wrestling with whether or not I should sit it out this time.

What do we do when we make plans, but life happens, getting in the way of our intended goal? When we have to get a new job, or move across the country, or care for a sick family member, or get sick ourselves? Do we give up on our dream, our passions, what we want our future to look like? Like death and taxes, change is a constant. Life is full of unexpected turns that cause us to reevaluate and recalibrate our plans. Instead of calling it quits, we adapt. Make adjustments. Lighten our load if necessary. Shift our priorities. But dealing with a life change or becoming limited to some degree doesn't mean not being able to do *any*thing.

It's always easier to come up with excuses than solutions. But when obstacles appear, it's usually not the end of the world. It doesn't mean our dreams have to die. It doesn't mean the future we are trying to create will never happen. It just means we might need to take smaller steps. Or maybe a few steps back or even in another direction. But this can still represent progress.

I finally realized that being pregnant wasn't a reason to give up a challenging hunt. Rather, it was another reason to reach for my goals and discover just how far hard work could take me. Over the years, I've learned how to focus and persevere in the face of obstacles. I've battled my insecurities about being a woman in the predominantly masculine world of hunting. I've fought through self-doubt, wondering if following my passion was worth it. But I've pushed through the resistance and become a stronger woman for it. So long as my doctor gave me the okay, I decided, *New Mexico, here I come.*

To prep for the hunt, I did some intense workouts—including hitting the stair climber with a heavy backpack and pushing sleds weighted down with hundred-pound plates. I did everything I could to prepare my body. I'll admit, it wasn't easy. Especially when I was knocked sideways by bouts of nausea, fatigue, and ligament pain. Plenty of times I would have much rather laid on the couch and watched Netflix all day. But I knew that the more hard work I put in, the more my future self would thank me.

When I arrived at hunting camp in the Gila National Forest in New Mexico, I definitely looked out of place. But even though I sported the biggest belly in the group (and had to wear my husband's camo shirt, because my regular hunting clothes were too tight), I felt pretty good. For sure, this was a physically demanding hunt. Hiking from dawn until dusk up steep mountains eight thousand feet above sea level, on rough terrain, requires strength, stamina, and muscle.

Most of the other hunters were in great shape, having also prepared for months without a baby growing inside them. Though I was tempted to compare my fitness level to that of everyone else at camp, I had to remain conscious of my own capabilities. I was focused on the health of my baby. I didn't care how quickly others got up the mountain, I would measure my progress using my own barometer.

In the spirit of transparency, I'll admit that, although I was there to hunt elk, my first priority on day one was just getting myself up to the top of the mountain. As expected, my pace was slower than usual, and I had to take frequent breaks to catch my breath and keep my heart rate in check. But on a crisp day in November 2016, I stood on the rocky peak of an eight-thousand-foot-high mountain overlooking cedar- and juniper-dotted slopes. As I took deep breaths, I felt my little girl kick and squirm in my womb. (We had learned her gender by then.) I was struck with awe. A life was forming inside me while I was enjoying a life I'd worked so hard to create. As I fixed my gaze on the amphitheater of cliff faces stretched out before me, I thought about my grandfathers, who had passed away. I was sad that my daughter would never get the chance to meet them, but I was grateful to be able to connect them through this pastime we all shared. Just as my grandfathers passed down their hunting stories to their children, I will do the same with my daughter.

The wind rushed through my hair as bold colors—brilliant blue from the sky, rich green from the trees—arched around me. The majestic beauty of the mountains brought me back to my first time hunting elk.

"Dinosaurs," I whisper. A chorus of otherworldly squeaks and squeals fills the woods, making me feel as if I'm walking through a live set from the movie *Jurassic Park*.

"Shh," Dad hisses. "We need to be quiet."

I listen more intently, playing detective to the piercing shrills that echo through the mountains. "Elephants? Sasquatch? Chimpanzees?"

"Eva, enough." Dad holds a hand in the air, putting a pin in my early-morning comedy routine.

As we're in the northwestern part of Colorado, I'm aware that elephants, chimpanzees, and dinosaurs are not the source of the sounds I hear in the predawn pitch-blackness. Likely, it's not Sasquatch, either. It's elk bugling. Sounds like hundreds of them. The whistling pitches overlap in a spine-tingling orchestral melody unlike anything I've ever heard. I have no clue where they're coming from. Acoustics on a timber-lined mountain are tricky. If a male elk, a bull, bugles while facing toward you, he'll sound closer than he really is. If he's facing in the opposite direction, he'll sound farther away.

Elk bugle for a lot of reasons. During the rut, they may bugle in frustration or to vocalize dominance over their herd of cows. My guide is an expert elk caller, well versed in bull bugles and cow calls. This is key to hunting these animals, which, during this time of year, prefer to hang out in dense timber instead of open fields.

The property on which we hunt belongs to a friend. Flatland doesn't exist here outside of what's under the hunting lodge perched on top of a hill 8,400 feet above sea level. But this five-thousand-plus-acre mountain paradise boasts some of the highest density of elk on the planet. It's not unusual to see more than a hundred of them in a day. Here's a neat fact: To preserve the beauty and abundance of the land, the owner put it into a conservation easement with the Rocky Mountain Elk Foundation. Because of this strategic partnership, the property will never be developed. Consequently, the wildlife can forever roam free.

In daylight, the near-autumn foliage here is spectacular. Vibrant reds collide with green pine and glowing gold, a bouquet of contrasts against a clear blue sky. But just before six in the morning, the sun is tucked neatly under the horizon, and all I can see are my guide's hiking boots as I follow his steps carefully. The owner of the property hikes behind me. Finally, we each park against a tree and wait for the sun to rise. The strategy for hunting here is simple: Listen for a bugling bull, spot it, and stalk it.

The blackness of the night lightens, opening unhurriedly the doors to dim light. Tiny droplets of dew cling to blades of grass and tree branches. Some of these drops tumble to the earth floor. As gray blankets the sky, I hear an elk bawling somewhere to the right of me, another up ahead. It's a non-stop soundtrack to the unveiling morning.

For hours that first day and the next, we trek up mountains, following the invisible trail of bugles. At one lookout point, I stand 9,900 feet in elevation, my lungs hard at work. No one says much as we stop and listen, but I'm afraid my wheezing and heavy breaths are a dead giveaway to our presence in this elk-drenched land. I'm used to long hikes and steep ascents, but it takes at least two days before my lungs get acclimated to this altitude.

At noon on day three, we break for lunch. It's quiet around midday. The elk bugling seems to die down as if on cue. Hey, even mating elk need a break. I chow down on soft granola bars and deer jerky. Crumbs sticking to my lips, I say to my guide, "Looks like these elk are done for the next few hours until it cools back down tonight. Nap time's calling my name."

"Yup. I'm not that far behind you."

"And once they're up and moving again, same plan as this morning?"

The guide nods. "That's right. We'll try to locate a mature, bugling bull and get as close as we can so he can hear my bugles and cow calls. Hopefully he'll give you a shot."

With an hour or two left before the vocal ensemble resumes their bugling anthem, my eyes start to feel heavy. Having slept for only a handful of hours the night before, my body craves shut-eye. "I'll be just over here if anyone needs me," I tell the group, pointing toward the bend around the mountain as I walk away.

Resting against a slender quaking aspen tree, white bark scarred with black, I'm out of sight from the hunting party. My knees sandwich a bulging backpack. I look up at the sky. In between the blazing yellow leaves that tremble gracefully in the breeze, fragments of sapphire pop out. I hear nothing but the wind whisking through the dancing gold as I fall into a deep sleep.

Forty-five minutes later, my face itches. Something is crawling on my cheek. Horrified, I swat at the hairy, long-legged spider I imagine is on my skin. One blink tells a different story. A deluge of gold leaves twirls down from the sky, and one or two have landed on my face. The sun slants through the trees, adding a shimmering veil to the shedding aspen. I am wonderstruck as the air bursts with yellow sparkles in free fall.

I stare at the leaves spinning in slow motion around me. Cupping my hands toward the sky, I let them rain down into my palms. The leaves are crisp and round, covering my skin with a film of gold. As I sit under the falling canopy of canary diamonds, the scent of autumn grows stronger with each descending leaf. It's one of the most beautiful displays of nature I've ever seen. I want to stay here forever. Basking in the shower of blazing yellow, I feel energized. Refreshed. I can barely feel the ache from the fifty-something miles my feet have traveled in the last three days. The rumbling in my belly is barely noticeable, either.

Marine biologist and author Rachel Carson wrote, "There is something infinitely healing in the repeated refrains of nature—the assurance that dawn comes after night, and spring after winter."[1] Being in the outdoors has forced me to check in with myself. Accustomed to a fast-paced life of constant travel, meetings, and events, I need to be outside, not just to harvest an animal that will feed my family, but to take an intentional opportunity to stop. To look. To listen. To breathe. I remind myself who's really in charge—God. Out in nature I can talk to Him without distraction. I can open the spiritual doors to my heart in a sanctuary that's protected from the rush of daily life. There are no phones here. No computers. No iPads. And the quiet pulls me closer to myself and closer to God.

Sometimes I wonder what would've happened if I'd never asked my father to teach me to hunt. Or what if his dad had never taught him? All these opportunities for me to stop, look, listen, and breathe deeply of nature would have been missed. As I sit here writing this final chapter, I am a month away from meeting my first child. As I think about my daughter and her life ahead, I hope she and her own children can continue to love the outdoors, appreciate fresh air, and be grateful for God's magnificent creation.

The cascade of yellow aspen leaves in Colorado continues for what seems like eternity. When the wind slows its pace and finally disappears, the last leaf falls onto the tip of my dirt-caked hiking boot. A faint bugle sounds. Then another. I'm almost at the end of my journey in the mountains. One that will leave behind another memory etched in my mind. Beauty rages all around me. She nudges me back to the place where, years earlier, I made the decision to hunt.

Choosing my own path has helped me reap rewards I otherwise would never have known. It's taught me to stay strong in my convictions even as others hurl death threats at me. It's enlarged my appreciation for every animal I harvest that will feed me, my family, and the many communities who rely on food donations. It's created a sense of wonder as I pause to behold the wind that rushes over water once as still as glass, the slope of a craggy mountain that's crowned with a halo of shimmering snow. It's made me thankful for generations past, remembering how I grasped the weathered hands of my grandfathers as we trekked through snow-covered prairie flats.

If you hunt, you might understand these sentiments. If not, I wonder if something you've read in this book has moved you. Maybe something is stirring in your soul. Maybe you've realized the passion you want to pursue. Maybe you've rekindled a desire you had long forgotten about. Maybe you've just uncovered the courage you need to pursue a dream. Listen to these inner voices. Trust your gut, and follow your heart. Don't turn back. You never know where you might end up.

Sometimes I wonder if I actually chose this path or if maybe, just maybe, this path chose me. Maybe I wasn't born with the desire to hunt, but somewhere along the line, the hunter was born in me.

After five hard days of hunting, I finally harvested an elk. And that night, when the last of the meat was packed up, I stared at the orange glow stretched out above the mountains. As I took a deep breath of fresh air, I wondered what new adventure lay ahead.

ACKNOWLEDGMENTS

Thank you to Esther and Whitney at the FEDD Agency, I never would have dreamed of tackling this project if it weren't for your encouragement and faith in me.

To all of the incredibly talented people at Penguin Random House, thank you for believing that my unusual story was worth sharing with the world and for your diligence and hard work during the process. Thank you Dave Kopp, for taking me on as your passion project. Derek Reed, your thoughtful insight was irreplaceable. Tina Constable, I haven't forgotten about the fishing trip we still need to take!

Thank you to A. J. Gregory, for leading me forward through every page of this book. Your endless energy, talent, and compassion were inspiring and uplifting. Thank you for sticking with me from start to finish.

To my long-time manager, Gregg Gutschow, I appreciate your advice and support in this process and throughout my career.

A special acknowledgment to my good friend, the late Dan Goodenow. Our adventures are some of my favorite memories—the Fun Box isn't nearly as fun without you.

Dad and Mom, this book is a testament to your job as

parents. I hope you can recognize all of the wisdom and love you shared along the way that molded me into who I am today. Dad, my research assistant, my fact checker, my hunting partner and mentor—thank you for opening my eyes to a world of wonder and being my champion. Mom, my best girlfriend, my role model, my cheerleader—thank you for keeping our family glued together and never wavering in your love and support, even when I chose the unexpected. And Bran, thanks for being my travel companion in the early years—our childhood was an unforgettable ride.

To my husband, Tim, from our first meeting in Raleigh, I have fallen more in love with you day after day. You are my touchstone, my rock, my whole heart—I can't imagine tackling this journey without you by my side.

And finally, the greatest gift from God, my daughter, Leni Bow. I was pregnant with you for the entire writing process of this book, and you were the inspiration to tell my story of perseverance in the face of adversity. As you grow up, I hope you feel the confidence to conquer the world, sweet girl. You can accomplish it all. You are strong, you are smart, you are already a beautiful soul in your tiny body. I love you now and forever.

NOTES

Introduction

1. Glenda Riley, *The Life and Legacy of Annie Oakley* (Norman, OK: University of Oklahoma Press; New edition, 2002), 143.

2. Randall Mueller, "Strong Growth in Female Hunting and Shooting Numbers," Real Tree Business Blog, November 3, 2015, business.realtree.com/business-blog/strong-growth-female-hunting-and-shooting-numbers.

I: My Normal

1. Fred R. Shapiro, *The Yale Book of Quotations* (New Haven: Yale University Press, 2006), 705.

3: Taking Aim

1. Brian Tracy, *Maximum Achievement* (New York: Simon & Schuster, 1995), 67.

2. Isak Dinesen, *Out of Africa* (New York: Modern Library, 1992), 4.

3. André Gide, *Autumn Leaves* (New York: Philosophical Library, 2011), https://tinyurl.com/z42jrqf.

4: The Longest Day

1. bartleby.com/90/1005.html.

2. nssf.org/PDF/HunterFactCard.pdf.

5: Into the Woods

1. Randy Pausch, *The Last Lecture* (New York: Hyperion, 2008), 149.

8: Haters Hate

1. Simon Paige, *The Very Best of Winston Churchill: Quotes from a British Legend* (CreateSpace, 2014), 15.

2. ncwildlife.org/Portals/0/Learning/documents/Species/Bear/NCWRC-BearManagementProgramBrochure.pdf.

3. Text of commencement speech given by Steve Jobs at Stanford University, June 12, 2005, news.stanford.edu/2005/06/14/jobs-061505.

4. "Russian women take aim in female hunting club," Reuters, November 9, 2015, https://tinyurl.com/gpog8k2.

5. nssf.org/share/pdf/GirlPower.pdf.

6. "Not Just One of the Guys: Why More Women are Hunting Than Ever Before," *Sporting Classics Daily,* February 2, 2015, https://tinyurl.com/jgvwpxk.

10: Diamonds from the Sky

1. *Rachel Carson, Legacy and Challenge,* Lisa Sideris and Kathleen Dean Moore, eds. (New York: Houghton Mifflin, 1962), 273.